METHODS OF PSYCHIC DEVELOPMENT

CW00551501

METHODS OF PSYCHIC DEVELOPMENT

DR. QUANTZ CRAWFORD

SAMUEL WEISER
York Beach, Maine

Published in 1982 by
Samuel Weiser, Inc.
Box 612
York Beach, Maine 03910

Reprinted 1988

ISBN 0-87728-545-4
Library of Congress Catalog Card No. 82-83876

Printed in the United States of America

CONTENTS

ILLUSTRATIONS

Dedicated to
THE GNOSTIC AQUARIAN SOCIETY

To all those persons who seek the Ancient and
Eternal Wisdom—The Gnosis—in this New Age.

INTRODUCTION

ESP! Everyone knows about ESP today. Why, it's a mark of intelligence, of being "informed," to even discuss it. Yes, you're literate! But yesterday, to even think of those things, some of which "ESP" stands for, or for which the words were coined, was to invite derision. You were not "all there," a little off, tetched, and all that sort of thing. Superstitious, even. It just wasn't mentioned in high society, nor even low society. The very idea that man could "see" without using his two physical eyes, or hear things not heard by others—why, he had to be a freak, or it was the work of the devil. If a man moved out of his physical covering it was considered epilepsy, or the "Holy Sickness." If he looked into a crystal or mirror, it was black magic, nonsense, or worse.

Yes, authorities just closed their eyes to the likes of people like Swedenborg, who described the distant fire and left his body at will, or Omar Khayaam ("I sent my soul through the Universe"), or the Bible statements "there is a psychic body and a natural body" (I *Cor.* 15:42) and "I know this man, whether in the body or out I know not" (II *Cor.* 12:2) and the many, many other testimonies recorded and related by man down through the centuries. Yes, that's the way to do it—close your eyes, close your mind, deny it, don't dare *believe* it, and it ipso facto ceases to exist, or to be so.

Nevertheless, all these things happen, and still more you've never heard about, whether the church, the authorities, your Aunt Fanny or any other know-it-all friend, relative, or otherwise admits it or not. And these things, these abilities, can be learned. They can be acquired through effort, practice and know-how—just like any other skill.

This book is designed for just that. There is no danger in any bit of it. It's all natural and normal, as normal and natural as the soul, or mind and its appendages, or energy.

For man is a Being, a consciousness. Basically, He IS. And as Being, he therefore is the product, the outflow of the universal ALL, a Spark from the all-pervading Flame, a ray of Light extended from the One Light, a note from the great "Lost Chord." This man then, became imbued with Mind, which serves as a tool—there we have the essence of man. Man has been described as a trinity, not only in Christianity but also in the Hindu, Buddhist, Egyptian and other religions. This trinity, as one, has been designated variously by people in different lands as ATMA-BHUDDHI-MANAS, OSIRIS-ISIS-HORUS, BRAHMA-VISHNU-SIVA, FATHER-SON-HOLY GHOST (HOLY as distinguished from the other lower and material ghosts as part of the makeup of man), and so on.

Thus Atma, Osiris, Brahma, Father, and so on are all the same, each referring to the 1st of the Trinity, "God," if you will. Buddhi, Isis, Vishnu, Son, are likewise equivalents, the first emanation of the ONE, the Supreme, the Spiritual Being—SOUL if one wishes to call it thus. One tries to avoid use of commonly used names because of such a diversity of understandings of a word. So we avoid the use of the word 'Christ' because of this reason. Manas (from which the word *mind* is derived), Horus, Siva, Holy Ghost, are also equivalents, all meaning MIND, which becomes the ego (but not in the sense that certain amongst people think of the word).

In each case, the first name represents the Great Unseen Parent, the all-pervading Consciousness; the second name is that of Man the Soul, the Son of the Source (God); and the third name the Mind, the Ego, the actor. Understand—we are not yet talking of bodies. Bodies are material things, subject to Maya. Remember, 'tis the *mind* that leads into bondage, and that same mind can lead one back to freedom. Thus man has to sojourn in this stratum of existence. So of necessity, like the chocolate-covered peanut, man was "dipped" and covered with mental substance as he went through this stratum, and with a lower, less vibrant, more material substance in the next lower stratum usually called the Astral; and then, at the "time" he is involved into a physical body, he grows, matures, sojourns and finally becomes evicted from this cumbersome covering at the end. This material covering contains, then, a semi-gross, fluid-like substance, the container of Energy ("authorities" said Mesmer was talking through his hat), which substance has been seen and can flow out from the flesh, under certain circumstances, and has been seized and analyzed in the laboratory. So there we have MAN in his entirety—a septenary, when we add the concept of Prana to the above.

For each of these bodies, or coverings, there are respective worlds, planes, strata or whatever, which the respective body is normal to and can function in, and the material of which they are made up of.

So we have A (the Supreme), B (man, the soul), C (the mind), and D, E, F, and G. At so-called "death," F and G are merely removed, let loose of, detached, discarded from A,B,C,D, and E. So everyone mourns, wails, suffers, and they spend hundreds of dollars on this worn-out or no-longer-useful covering (the overcoat), place it in the cold, wormy ground, put flowers on its grave—the depository of this detached hunk of material *garment*—beneath an expensive stone marker. What would you think of yourself if you acted this way toward an old overcoat after it was worn out, useless, and no longer desirable—putting it into an expensive box, placing it in ground bought for a fat fee, buying flowers for it and crying over it? This is what people are in reality doing.

Now we have "ABCDE" free from its leaden weight, functioning on E plane (astral), no longer seen (ordinarily) by the fleshly, and if and when seen, scaring H---out of whoever "sees" (a ghost no less!). Why? John Doe is the same person as when wearing his "overcoat" of flesh. No real difference.

After awhile another "coat" becomes detached, E, (the astral) which then leaves just ABCD (the old Bible spoke of the *three* coats of skin). Now ABCD is no longer "seen" and no longer is it so easy to make contact. Picture three rooms in a house: room #1, the physical flesh world; room #2 and room #3, room #2 being between #1 and #3. Room #2 is the Astral world or plane, the plane of E, and room #3 is the plane of D, the plane of mental matter. So now ABCD exists in this world of mental matter, a world of happiness, where LIGHT is everywhere, the heavenworld about which you hear so much spoken. This is where the "unliving" abide, until—. (The Book of Job speaks of the Soul "rising" or "returning" again into the light of the living—). There is a fourth world, a higher plane, but ABCD usually never knows about this world, and couldn't get there anyway unless prepared while still in FG, the world of flesh, and to get into the Fourth World, one would have to leave behind D, even if only temporarily.

The Causal body is called so because this is where all our trouble starts. The problems of the Astral body and then the physical body are engendered (caused) in the mental *Body*, so, causal Body. To recapitulate the above, we have first the Trinity:

A—the Supreme. "The unseen Parent of the Soul", as it has been written in an Eastern source.

B—Man (Real) (the Christos) (Buddhic Splendor) SOUL.

C—Mind (not 'mental'),
and then we have:

D—Mental Body (Causal Body), the first of the three "Coats of Skin" as it used to be called in the *old* bible. (The *old* bible is the one from which the first translators got their material and translated from, and through their ignorance *mis*translated so much.)

E—Astral Body, so called because of the trillions of Stars seen when it is seen by the seeing one.

F—The Etheric Double, a body semi-material, fluidic in nature (the substance of which was analyzed chemically by Sir Prof. Crooks and referred to by spiritualists as Ectoplasm—the substance which flowed out from Palladino, the medium), the Body which is the *container* of "Life of the Body," "Energy," like a bag, so to speak.

The reason or the secret why some live so long is that age is the consequence of this "bag" not being replenished every night, or else becoming "worn" so that it can't retain the *life* that it receives from the Source of Life. It may be likened to the thin skin that adheres to the egg shell, for never should the twain be separated.

G—The Physical, gross, material body we all are acquainted with so well, and mistakenly call Man, and mistakenly call 'Me', 'I', etc. FG is really a unit in itself. F follows the carcass to the grave, and can be seen (by some) in its more vapory aspect, hovering over the dead bodies at *night* in graves.

Now in this book we are going to learn ways and means of becoming cognizant of these things and learn the means of acquiring abilities possible and available to any normal person. There is no one to hold you back but yourself. You will be given the way to develop this respectable ESP and also to go out from your physical covering, from your overcoat, and function in your *suit* (astral), and sometime maybe to even function in your *underclothing* (mental substance body). It's up to you. Fear not. Be not discouraged by anyone.

Relating to each of these levels or planes, we have psychic centers, chakras, as they've been called. First, we have the basic center (muladhara), the home of Kundalini, and relating to the Etheric plane and substance. Above this is the Astral center, Svadisthana, and the Solar Plexus center (Manipura), which relates to the mental body. Then there is the Heart center (Hridaya) relating to mind itself (Manas) and of the Fourth World, the first plane of the Spiritual worlds itself. Below these are the planes of Matter in its descending and increasing degree of material density. Above the Heart center is the throat center (Visudha) connected to the world or plane of ether. Ajna, the center between the eyes, relates to the Soul or Spirit itself, the real person himself. Sahasra, or the crown center at the top, relates to the highest Consciousness. Each of these centers confers functions and abilities respective to each plane from levitation, projection, mind reading and clairvoyance to other even more unusual capacities.

The Kundalini, called by the Greeks "Spierema," is the power-energy residual at Muladhara, which must be awakened, increased, and raised. This accomplishment is spoken of and taught amongst all nations, all people, in all times. Any method used, in time, must bring this about for ultimate accomplishment.

Know, dare, and be silent. Carry on.

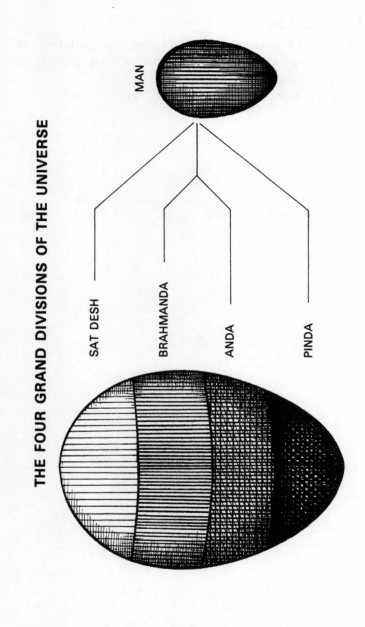

THE FOUR GRAND DIVISIONS OF THE UNIVERSE

MAN

SAT DESH

BRAHMANDA

ANDA

PINDA

PHILOSOPHY

In order to understand words, names, ideas, concepts, and the functioning of Man, it is well to become acquainted to some degree with the Philosophy underlying the subject with which we are dealing.

THE FOUR GRAND DIVISIONS OF NATURE. The universe is divided into four grand sections, each marked out and differentiated from the others by certain characteristics of the substances composing them and the nature of the phenomena to be seen there.

Beginning with our world, the first grand division is the physical universe, called PINDA. It is composed of matter, as we know, of varying density, coarse in quality; but mixed with a very small percentage of mental and spiritual substance, just enough to give it life and motion. Without spirit, matter is dead, inert. In fact, there is nothing in all creation wholly devoid of spirit. To enable us to get some grasp upon the situation, suppose we imagine the pre-creation substance to have existed somewhat in the form of an egg. The large end of this egg may be thought of as the positive pole, in which the original substance existed and still exists in a highly concentrated form. So it is polarized. The small end is the negative pole, in which the same substance exists in a less concentrated form. In the process of creation, the smaller end, or negative pole, becomes—not separated, but differentiated from the original mass, and then subdivided into three distinct portions. The uppermost of these subdivisions is BRAHMANDA, the middle portion is ANDA, and the nethermost one is PINDA, the physical universe. All of this end of creation, this lower section, is composed of coarse matter, while the higher sections are much finer in substance as one advances to higher regions. This section has a much lower rate of vibration than any section above it.

As said above, the grand division just above the physical universe is called the ANDA. The word means egg, referring to its shape. If we must place it in space, let us assume that ANDA lies just above and beyond the physical universe. However, in reality all these higher worlds are separated from this one more by their ethereal qualities than by location in space. The substance of ANDA is much finer in the structure of its atoms, in its vibratory activity and its degree of density. ANDA is also much more vast in extent than the physical universe. The central portion of that universe makes up what is commonly spoken of as the astral plane. In this grand division we have an endless variety of life, here we have many so-called heavens (they really are not *Heaven*) and here we have the purgatories.

Next above the ANDA lies BRAHMANDA, the third grand division. This term means the "egg of Brahma." It is also egg-shaped, like ANDA, but is still much more vast in extent. It is also more refined and full of light, than either Anda or the physical universe. This third grand division is composed mostly of spirit substance, but is mixed with a refined sort of matter. And Anda contains more of spirit substance than Pinda, in like manner, Brahmanda is richer in spirit than is Anda. In fact, spirit predominates in Brahmanda, just as matter predominates in Pinda. Anda is rather on the dividing line between the two.

Last of all we arrive at the highest grand division in all creation, the finest and purest, composed entirely of pure spirit. This region is definitely beyond the sphere of matter. There is no mind in this region. The plane of Universal Mind is the lower end of Brahmanda. This is excluded from the supreme grand division. The lower end of Brahmanda is made up almost entirely of mind substance. In this last and highest grand division we discover the region of Universal Spirit. Its name is SAT DESHA which means the abiding or real country. It is the region of truth, of ultimate reality. The light in this world is so extremely intense that no man on earth can form any conception of it. Here we find PURUSHA, the LORD of this spiritual region. This is but one name of the Supreme. But then there are Lords of the lower regions, Kal being the "overlord" of the negative planes, the worlds of matter.

MAN AND HIS SEVERAL PARTS.

Beginning with the lower stratum, we may say first of all that man is an animal. He is a physical body called in the East ISTHUL SHARIRA. This body, as we know, is subject to all the frailties of matter as well as influences from higher or more subtle sources.

Then there is another body inside and interpenetrating through this physical man, a much finer body, called the SUKHSMA SHARIRA, (subtle body), or NURI SARUP, (light body). It is commonly called the Astral body because, when seen, it appears to sparkle with millions of little particles resembling star dust. It is much ligher and finer than the physical body. This body every person possesses and uses here and now, although he may be unconscious of it. It is through this body that the mind and soul are able to make contact with the physical body and the outside world. This finer body takes shape in harmony with the character of the individual. On that plane no deception is possible. Everyone is seen just as he is. The astral body has its five senses, just like the physical body. When the physical body dies, this finer body remains as the instrument of expression upon that higher plane of life.

Inside and through this Astral body, and quite distinct from it, there still is another 'material' body, much finer and more subtle than the Astral. This body is called KARANA SHARIRA. That means the causal body. So named because it is the real cause, and embodies the seed of all that will ever take place in that individual's life. It has also been called BIJ SHARIRA, which means 'seed body.' This body is as much finer than the Astral, as the Astral is finer than the physical. This body is usually called the *mental body* in the west. It may be regarded as a portion of the mind itself, acting as a sort of sheath around the soul. Its function is to receive and transmit impressions between the mind and soul on one side, and between the mind and the Astral body on the other. In this body a perfect record is left of every experience of the individual, running through all of the times of its existence. If one is able to read those records, he can see what that man has done or had done to him during his entire past. And also what he is going to do in the future! It is all there, the future in seed form, the past in visible record. The KARANA SHARIRA is man's highest and finest instrument of action, except for the mind itself.

The MIND is the fourth unit in the construction of man. As has been already noted, it is so closely related to the mental body that it is not easy to distinguish between them. Both the MIND and the mental body are derived from the Universal Mind. The mind is something finer than the KARANA SHARIRA or mental body, more subtle, and in closer proximity to the soul itself. Because of this proximity, it is also endowed with much greater powers.

So long as we are in the material regions (i.e.the World of Matter, including the physical, the Astral and mental levels), we must retain the mind and the KARANA SHARIRA. If we are to manifest on the astral plane, we must also have both the Karana Sharira and the Sukhsma Sharira, the Causal and Astral bodies. Naturally, we must also have the physical body if we are to manifest here on the plane of physical matter. When the individual rises from the physical to the Astral, then the Causal, and finally leaves the Causal on his upward journey, he discards all three instruments, because he no longer needs them—because the donkey cannot fly with the bird, and the bird cannot go so high as the Eagle. Realize this can take place without "Death" of the physical. When he reaches the region above the causal, and above the mental or mind world itself, he finds himself clear of all instruments, and beholds himself as pure SPIRIT. This region is known as DASWAN DWAR.

We need all these bodies for consciousness to use and intercommunication between Man the Spirit and Man the flesh. Besides, whether we want it or like it or not, we "reside" in the mental (causal) level between Embodiments. It is Here where the Skandhas (we don't have an appropriate English word to fit the meaning) are 'unhitched,' so to speak, 'disassociated,' and are re-associated when time of rebirth begins to take place. You might liken the Skandhas to the Electrons, the material of the astral to the atoms, and that of Flesh to Molecules. So when being reborn we take on the mental matter; then, when passing through the Astral we get another 'coating' encapsulated with astral matter, and then are 'sucked' into the Flesh Body with its Etheric Substance F (see previous chapter) at birth.

It may be difficult for us to understand how a person can discard his mind and still know anything. This is only because we have been so accustomed to regard mind as the instrument of knowing. But as a matter of fact, it is not the mind that knows. Mind alone is as powerless to know as is an automobile. It is but another instrument used by the soul. It is the SOUL alone that does the actual knowing. For this reason, when the Soul rises into Daswan Dwar and above, it has no need of the mind or any of the material bodies. It knows by direct perception.

If you ever have the privilege of seeing your real spiritual nature, you will see a FIRE MIST. In point of TIME the Fire Mist was given a Mind, and then we became a trinity. (See Blavatsky's reference to Sons of the Fire Mist.)

Last of all we come to the real man, the soul, the very core of his being, the fifth unit in the construction of his being. Remember, man has all five of these elements while living here now. But all of the lower instruments are discarded, one by one, or put in abeyance, as he advances upward. This is because he has no further use for them on the higher planes, each instrument being suited for expression only upon a particular plane of life. The Soul is the real man, the Jiv-Atman as it is called in the East. The individual Soul is a spark from the INFINITE LIGHT, a drop from the ocean of being. As such it is ONE WITH HIM, one in substance, one in qualities. It is in the soul that all consciousness resides. And all power. The Soul is permeated by the essence of Him; He is in and of the Soul as the Soul is in and of Him, just as the drop of water is in and of the ocean, and the ocean is in and of the drop of water. I AND THE FATHER ARE ONE.

SYMBOL OF MAN

THE AURA

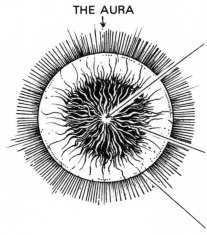

THE UNSEEN PARENT OF THE SUN (SON). THE *A* OF AUM. GOD, ATMA, BRAHMA, OSIRIS, THE FATHER ATON, ALLAH, SOUL OF THE SOUL.

THE SUN (FIRE MIST), THE SON OF GOD. THE *U* OF AUM. CHRIST, BUDDHA, SELF, SOUL, ISIS, VISHNU, I.

MIND, THE *M* OF AUM. MANAS, SIVA, EGO, HORUS, HOLY GHOST.

SYMBOL OF MAN *IN* HIS BODY(S)

(THE SQUARE REPRESENTS THE FOUR BODIES)

CONCENTRATION

In speaking of concentration, we do not use the word as it is usually used in the West. The Western idea of concentration usually alludes to the complete devotion of attention to some endeavor, putting your whole effort into the project. The concentration that we refer to as it is done in the East and in Occult work is just as the word says—with centration. In other words, you center your entire consciousness and mind upon one thing and hold it there without deviation. One can, in the Western idea of concentration, be doing something with his so-called concentration abilities, and yet his mind can be all over the place while doing this.

In occult concentration, we strive to develop the ability of holding our mind, our attention, our consciousness on one place or on one idea. In doing this, there are several methods that are used by different teachers in different schools.

One method is the use of imagining a five-pointed star, with the point up. Or some other image may be used. In doing this you picture, or image, a five-pointed star at the center of the forehead, just above the root of the nose, and keep imaging, picturing, visualizing this five-pointed star, holding your attention there constantly—five, ten, fifteen minutes—without deviation or interruption. This isn't going to be easy at first; you will have to just keep trying, as your mind will wander. Every time it does, just bring it back; keep imaging that five-pointed star. This is perhaps a difficult way to develop concentration, but on the other hand it brings efficient results.

Another very good method involves the setting up of one center outside of the body and one inside of the body. First make a yellow spot on a white piece of paper; place it on a table or hang it on the wall level with the eyes. Sitting in solitude, do what is called *tratack*; fix the gaze on that spot. Keeping your attention on this yellow spot, gradually let your entire consciousness be absorbed into it. After this is practiced for a few weeks, the yellow spot is then changed to green and then into red and later into blue, and finally into purple or lavender. The object of the *tratack* practice, or spot gazing, is to have a clear vision of the elemental colors which are the representative colors of ether, earth, fire, and water or air. Developing perception of those colors relates you to one of those tatvic forces, powers, centers, which are gradually brought into play and activity. The purpose of visualizing in gazing at the colors, combines two things. Concentration and the *effect* of the color upon the system, as each color used is related, vibrates one of the centers, respective to each color. Thus the centers are related to respective Elements and energies and forces.

Muladhara relates to Earth—yellow—and earthy energies.

Svadisthana relates to Water—green—and astral energies.

Manipura to Red—Fire—mental energies.

Heart to Air—blue—mind.

Throat to Ether (not the chemical, but the fifth Element)—violet—and to something I won't give in a book.

Also, there are *shapes* related to each of these.

For quick results, this is to be done for at least two or three hours every day. It helps the eyesight a great deal and serves as a great aid in influencing others.

Again, one has to take care of the distance between the spot and the organ of sight. To begin with, the spot is to be located at a distance of two feet from the eye, and after practice, such as at the end of each week, the distance is to be reduced to one and a half feet, and then to one foot, and then to half a foot, and then to the root of the nose, which in fact becomes the real sadhana. This tratack develops into an exhilerating absorption. The importance of this is that the Vrittis (mental modulations) are to be controlled, or restrained from being 'scattered,' wandering from thought to throught, and instead collected, held, at the "still point" in the body. The mind is turned inwards, so to speak, just as it is mentioned in Buddhist writings, and others, and in time this brings the mind into contact with the Inner Sound called Nada, Word, NAAM, Shabd. This brings into activity and play the Pranas with their respective bestowments. (Prana is Energy, the sum-total of the Energies in the Universe, the sum-total of all the forces in the Universe, the Prime Vibration, having its source in the Eternal Source). By this process of tratack the mind and the pranas get into harmony and the soul escapes from the covering of the sheath. This process of decreasing the distance of the color spot is to be repeated with each color. One should continue the concentration on each of the colors after reaching the root of the nose for another four weeks.

Another very useful practice and an easier one in the method of developing concentration is that which the Buddhists make use of wherein you concentrate on the Nose Door as it is called. In this practice, you commence with the watching of the breath—as the breath comes in the nose, and goes out you *feel* it. You don't follow the breath at first, you just watch at the nose door, feel the breath come in, feel the breath go out.

After the practice of this for a period of a few weeks or months, you then *follow* the breath into the Heart area, follow the breath out to the nose door, follow the breath into the Heart area from the nose door, follow the breath out from the Heart area to the nose door. You practice this then for several weeks or months, as your case may need, until you are ready to go to the next stage wherein you merely concentrate at the nose door without thought as to the breath at all. In time you reach what is known as the *after image*. It may be a color, it may be a sound that you hear; it is some *experience*. Then you put your attention on *that*. Do not get the idea that you have quickly reached the *after image,* for it will take *several years* to reach this, with constant, consistent practice of this exercise.

All this is *anapani sati.* It starts with watching the breath at the nose door, leads into the other steps automatically, and finishes with the "After Image," which then becomes the concentration for the rest of the spiritual aspiration.

It may be the Voidness of Mahamudra. It may be one of several things.

Finally, one of the best methods of concentration—and this is to be used in conjunction with the concentration, at the root of the nose—is to add the repetition of some word with the ingoing and outgoing breath, while also imaging the particular color. One of the easiest words that you can repeat *mentally,* while concentrating at the root of the nose and on the color, is *hang-so.* This is mentally repeated as the breath comes in and the breath goes out. As the breath comes in, mentally say "So," and as the breath goes out, say mentally, "Hang." You don't force your breathing in any way. Just let the breath come and go as it will. You do this practice anywhere from fifteen minutes to a half hour. This is a very important part of the use of the spot concentration. The repetition of this word, or others, is one of the best systems of concentration.

Or, if one wishes, one can use the Buddhist mantra while concentrating at the root of the nose—OM MANI PADME HUM—pronounced:

OM—like "om" in the word "home."

MA—like "maw," or the "a" as sounded in the word "law."

NI—like in the word "knee."

PAD—same sound as above in the word "maw" or "law."

ME—sounded as in the word "maybe," or like the sound in the word "made."

HUM—sounded as in the word "whom," "room," or "moon."

This, then, is repeated over and over like a mental rosary, while concentrating at the root of the nose. This is used by thousands of Buddhist mystics very effectively.

These concentration practices, or the combination of them, will lead you to perfection in concentration and make you ready for the practice of meditation. You can't properly meditate until you are able to concentrate. Also following the ability to concentrate are other things you will do in the occult field. This ability in the proper manner is a *sin qua non*. So practice concentration; it is the key to all further occult progress.

MEDITATION

Man epitomizes the three grand divisions of the Universe. Thus, he has a spirit, or soul, which is linked to the related spiritual division; a mind, of the mental plane, related to the universal mind; the physical body, of the material plane, consisting of three bodies—the causal, the astral, and the gross or flesh body.

The gross body is merely the fleshly sheath we have, consisting of gross matter, gross organs, and senses. This is shaken off, discarded only, at death so-called.

The astral body consists of subtle matter and subtle organs but still matter no less. The physical body is but the duplicate of the astral pattern.

The causal body is the root cause of the other two lower material bodies. This is the mental body, made up of a mental matter. Its activity is confined to the deep sleep state. The latter two bodies along with the mind continue to exist after death and create a new form or physical frame at each rebirth.

Thus in man, we have the three grand divisions of the universe represented. The first is the region of truth and pure spirit, unmixed with matter. Here, the spirit reigns free and there is total absence of matter. This is the region where the Lord Himself dwells and may be defined as the purely spiritual region. This is the region and plane free from death and destruction. Whomsoever reaches this plane obtains true salvation, and true salvation is attained only by reaching this plane. This region has been called the abode of everlasting joy and peace.

The second grand division consists of pure spirit and a subtle form of matter combined in varying degrees. The upper part of it is called, in India, PARABAMAND; it is mostly spirit in substance, but is mixed with a certain amount of pure spiritualized matter. It is the finest order of matter. This is called the Spiritual-Material region, because Spirit dominates the region. As we descend toward the negative Pole of creation, the substance of this division gradually becomes less and less concentrated. The lower portions become coarser in particle and more and more mixed with matter. In the lower end of Brahmanda, Mind is supreme. Tirkuti, the lowest section of Brahmanda, is the home of Universal Mind. This region undergoes a change at the destruction of the Universe in the grand dissolution. A man in this region is safer than in the one below it.

The third division comprises spirit and matter in their grossest form, and is called the ANDA, the sphere of Maya. In this region, matter has the upper hand; spirit is subordinate to matter to such an extent that it becomes dependent on matter for its manifestation. In ANDA the spirit, on account of its association with matter, undergoes untold miseries and is subjected to the laws of transmigration. The second and the third divisions are under the rule of KAL and MAHAKAL respectively.

In going upward through the pursuance of the meditation practice, after rising above the body consciousness, you find yourself hemmed in by matter all around in ANDA, the third grand division. Then in rising into BRAHMAND, the region of the universal mind, you will feel much better.

This in brief is a sketch of the macrocosm, the great world Universe. These three divisions also exist in man on a miniature scale. If you want to know about the macrocosm, you must first know about the microcosm.

In the performance of the meditation, it is advisable to construct a meditation prop consisting of a piece of wood of the length of your torso from the base of the spine to the armpits. Across the top is nailed a cross-piece on which you can place your arms while you are stopping your ears so that your arms will not grow tired. You will have to take the measurements for your particular body so that the arms are put on a comfortable level. When you are sitting this way place the base of the prop either on the chair or on the floor where you might be sitting so that you have a comfortable position in which to perform your meditation.

Meditation is a subject or idea that is grossly misunderstood in the West. You hear various ideas relating to meditation wherein one is to meditate on a beautiful sunrise, or some beautiful poem or passage of some writing, or the vastness of the universe, or your relationship to or with the universe, placing yourself somewhere up in space with space all around you. In such concepts of meditation, one can "meditate" for five hundred years or an eternity and never experience any degree of inner development. Meditation is definitely another facet and necessary procedure in the attainment of inner development.

Meditation, as we in the West understand it, is to be completely forgotten and disregarded. Set aside all the ideas or concepts you have heretofore associated with meditation. Simply do the practices that are described below, which are classic exercises as taught by the esoteric schools, and designed to afford direct perception of the experience.

MEDITATION PROP

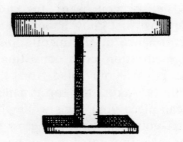

MEDITATION POSTURE

The first meditative exercise that we will learn is one
that is related to the spinal cord or channel. You are to sit
with the spine straight but relaxed and comfortable, with
nothing binding in your clothing. Sit either in a
straight-backed chair or on a small cushion with your back
braced so that it is straight, or crosslegged, or in a yoga
sitting posture if you can hold it comfortably for a
reasonable length of time, and be unaware of your body.
Then put your attention at the very bottom of the spinal
cord. You already know what concentration is, so apply
this technique in meditation. Concentrate all your
attention in the hollow channel of the spinal cord. Feel a
sensation of coolness, like a current of cool air, in this
channel; bring it up the spine; feel it rising up the spine to
the very top and into the head. Bring the current to the
center between the eyes at the root of the nose. Now go
back down the spine, concentrating on the feeling of a
current of heat descending the spine, back down to the
very tip. Then repeat, coming back up as if you were
lifting a cool current up the channel, as if there were a
hollow channel in your cord, which there is, and that you
are lifting a cool stream of air or energy or substance up
your spine. Up, up, up, straight up and into your head, to
the center between your eyes, then back down, down
instead, feeling a heat current; feel heat, you can feel it.
Imagine the heat current coming down the spine, back
down to the tip of the spine at the bottom. You repeat
this up-and-down, with these two opposite types of
feeling, for five minutes.

In the next meditation exercise, center all your
consciousness within the spinal cord itself. Put your whole
attention there—you are to forget all about the rest of
your body—your legs, your arms, your head, your eyes,
anything. Put forth all of your attention and try to make
the effort to seem as though you yourself were within the

ALTERNATE POSTURE
FOR MEDITATION

HANDS POSITIONED AS PICTURED OR
THEY MAY BE FOLDED IN FRONT

spine, as if you were the spine itself. Now with this idea
you image a light, a golden light streaming all the way up
your spinal channel, and as you image that, hold the
attention on that image, constantly holding it without
deviating. Let the golden light be there, holding it from the
tip of your spine to your eyes and then meditate on feeling
that light expanding; expand it, feel it expanding and
expanding, so that instead of feeling just a thin thread of
golden light you feel it expand to the width of the spinal
cord itself, to the diameter of an inch. Image this. This
cannot all be done in just a day or five minutes. Take time.
Start off with a meditation image of this thin cord, this
thin thread of golden light, and do this for a week, or two
weeks, or three or four; then go to the expansion step,
expanding it as you concentrate. Start with the thread and
expand it to the size of the cord itself, perhaps an inch in
diameter, and in time continue to expand it. You can
increase this expansion. Meditate on this golden light
expanding outwardly—enlarging and enlarging and
enlarging—so that after a few months you can expand this
light to the extent of your whole body, as if your whole
body were the spinal channel and nothing but golden light.
Start at the spinal cord and expand it outward until it
reaches the width of your body, until your whole body is
golden light. Then hold this meditation. In time you will
actually feel it. Just meditate, image, this concept as if you
were the spinal cord, as if you were enclosed and
enraptured, enwrapped, clothed in this golden light. This
will go a great way and bring a great amount of activity,
and produce an extensive influence upon your psychic
development. I would do this meditation upon the golden
light for about ten to fifteen minutes, then proceed to the
head area, using the following meditation. This consists of
closing the ears with the thumbs, closing the little tragus at
the ear. Put your thumbs on the outside and close your

ears so that you hear no sounds—the right thumb on the right ear opening, the left thumb on the left ear opening. Then, either close your hands or extend the fingers up over the head, but not so that the fingers touch each other over the top of the head. Then put your whole attention on or at the right ear. Listen. You are to listen, listen to the sounds that you will hear in the right ear. In the beginning you may no doubt hear nothing in particular, but you listen. At first, you may hear the sounds of blood rushing through the inner part of the head in the ear area, or you may hear other sounds, body noises, but pay no attention to these. In the course of time, if you continue to listen, you will fine that a subtle, subtle sound will be heard, perhaps like the buzzing of bees, or perhaps like the sound of a bell or many bells, or like that of high tension wires that you heard on a cold, cold day, when they hum. You might hear various sounds. The various scriptures like "The Voice of the Silence" by Blavatsky, the Upanishads, or the Bible describe these sounds or mention them. There are usually ten different sounds mentioned, but you pay no attention to these. You listen for sounds such as a roar of the Ocean, or a bell ringing, or thunder, or bees buzzing. In time one of these sounds will come. Some perhaps hear one sound first, then another; others may hear a different sound first. When this sound comes, put your whole attention on it, and in doing this you become "baptised." It is like jumping into a stream or current and getting immersed in it. It is like an elevator that lifts you. The sound is coming from above, actually, and in time it will lift your consciousness, your being, your nature, your soul, higher and higher toward God and the higher realms. This particular system is the only means of returning to our source, to the Oversoul. It is the actual, ancient, royal pathway to God. It is one of the most important practices that you learn and one of the most important that you do. This practice should be done for fifteen minutes to half an hour twice a day.

PSYCHIC ISOMETRICS

We all have heard of "isometrics" wherein there is tension exerted upon various groups of muscles, leading to their increased strength and development. The idea is not new; it was known many thousands of years ago in India, only it was called 'hatha yoga'. Not so commonly known is the fact that there are also isometric exercises for the development of the psychic centers.

The isometric exercise for the development of the Muladhara Chakra (center) is given in chapter 12; whereby you sit on the floor, contract your rectal region tightly with tension and lift yourself off the floor up and down while holding the contraction and doing that ten times as instructions are given.

For the next center above, known as Svadisthana, you lie down on the floor or in bed and swish your belly from right to left, sideways, left, right, left, right. Just swish your whole belly sideways, without interruption. To do this right you will find that you are moving your spine, too, at a certain area between the sacrum and lumbars. You are in fact exercising an area in that particular region in the performance of this exercise. Do this shaking 50 times, without stop, as an exercise. This enlivens the nerve center of psychic function, called the svadisthana.

For the Manipura, the third center, you sit up, spine straight, and lift your whole chest and the contents of your belly; really try to lift it. Lift your diaphragm,

THE CHAKRAS

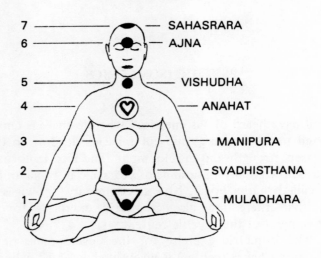

7 — SAHASRARA
6 — AJNA
5 — VISHUDHA
4 — ANAHAT
3 — MANIPURA
2 — SVADHISTHANA
1 — MULADHARA

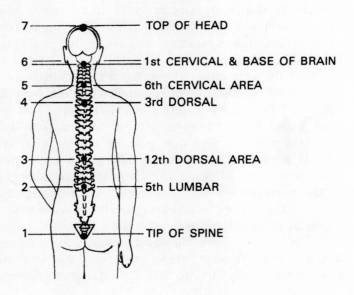

7 — TOP OF HEAD
6 — 1st CERVICAL & BASE OF BRAIN
5 — 6th CERVICAL AREA
4 — 3rd DORSAL
3 — 12th DORSAL AREA
2 — 5th LUMBAR
1 — TIP OF SPINE

pushing upward with your muscles, pulling upward toward your shoulders, upward, holding that tension for a count of ten and then let it down. Then do it again, pulling up your diaphragm, pulling up the bottom part of the chest, trying to pull it up toward your shoulders, pulling up and pulling in; all this is done by way of the muscles in the area, not with your hands in any way. You feel as if your belly is being pulled up. You do this again and again about ten times, holding for a count of ten each time.

For the center known as Anahat, the Heart center, you lie upon the floor and do pushups—yes, the old conventional pushups. So you raise and lower your body in this manner, doing this about fifteen times. Each time you raise your body, hold it that way, taking a deep breath each time you perform the exercise. When you let yourself down take another deep breath, push up and hold it there. You take a deep breath with each one of these exercises. Before you do the muladhara exercise you take a deep breath and swish your belly. When you do the manipura, take a deep breath and pull your chest up.

Then for the throat, the Vishudha center, take a deep breath and rotate your head around and around from the left. Circle down to the right shoulder, then back up to the first position, with the head straight up. And again, lean the head toward the left shoulder, circle down, toward the middle; then circle toward the right shoulder, and back to the straight-up position. Do this twenty times. Then reverse, and do the same exercise twenty times circling the opposite direction. Hold your breath all the while as you are doing the twenty circles.

Following these exercises, sit straight, contract the rectal region and just hold the contraction-tension. Tense this area and just hold it that way steadily for a period of three minutes. Put your attention at each of these areas while doing the tensions. Then contract the muscles in the

PSYCHIC ISOMETRICS

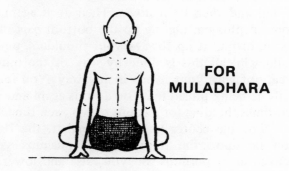

**FOR
MULADHARA**

FOR SVADHISTHANA

SWISH BELLY SIDEWAYS, LEFT TO RIGHT TO LEFT,
BACK & FORTH

LIFT CHEST.
DIAPHRAGM &
ABDOMINAL
MUSCLES

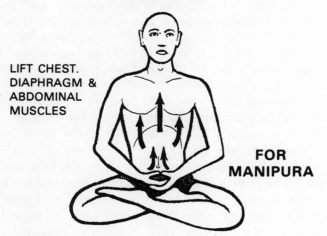

**FOR
MANIPURA**

PSYCHIC ISOMETRICS (CONT.)

FOR ANAHAT

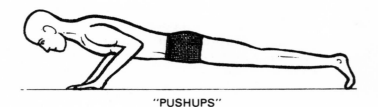

"PUSHUPS"

FOR VISHUDHA

FOR VISHUDHA ISOMETRICS: CIRCLE HEAD TO THE
LEFT, TO DOWN, TO THE RIGHT, TO ERECT, ETC.

area of the small of the back, holding this for the same length of time. Next, contract the muscles in the area where the ribs end at the spine and hold that—same length of time. Then flex your shoulders back, tense the muscles in the shoulder area behind the heart and hold the tension. Finally, tense and hold the muscles where the neck meets the shoulders and hold three minutes.

This will comprise your exercises in psychic isometrics. This is a preliminary or basic form. It has, of course, definite results in the awakening of your psychic centers. You should do all of these exercises in a schedule, in proper sequence. You will find all of them put together will speed your progress.

CENTER DEVELOPMENT

We have in our bodies several centers having to do with our psychic nature. These centers are also known in physiology and are given other functions in the physical body. However, they also have certain psychic functions which ordinary anatomy is not acquainted with. In all psychic development and in all people who have any kind of psychic ability, there are one or more particular psychic centers awakened in varying degrees. As part of your process in psychic development you therefore make use of concentration upon these particular centers. Each one of the centers has certain cosmic abilities or powers inherent in them. In other words, you acquire certain results or certain capacities of function by the awakening of these particular centers.

One center has to do with the leaving of the body, another center has to do with the seeing and hearing aspect, or the will power. Some centers have to do with particular levels of consciousness so that your lower centers can get you in contact with your lower types of consciousness; your higher center, of course gets you in contact with your higher nature, so that you have one center that relates to the mind in such a way that you get mindreading capacities. You have another center that relates you with your causal body, usually called the mental body, *karana sarira*. You have one center that relates to the astral body and you have one center that relates to the power of Word, and so on. In most mediums, you will find that the centers that give them the ability of doing what they do are either the partially awakened basic center or the awakening solar plexus center. They very rarely have any of the higher centers developed; that's why they have a negative phase of development.

Materialization mediums are those who have the lowest center partially awakened so that it allows ectoplasm to flow out of the body and produce materializations and various material phenomena: teleportation, levitation, etc.

Of the lower centers (i.e. the Basic and Svadisthana), perhaps the second center is the one that enables them to see the "spooks," as people usually call them, or what they conceive of as entities of the departed souls. So in our development as part of the processes of the psychic development, we will now take up each one of these centers in turn and show you how to do this.

The first of three to be concentrated on is the solar plexus. We all know where the solar plexus is. It is down there in the region of the navel; so you just put your attention at the navel area and visualize light. Just image a light there. Concentrate your whole attention on the navel or the solar plexus area, all the while holding the image of a light at that center. Concentrate there; concentrate. Exclude all other thinking. Keep holding your thought at the solar plexus navel center. This practice is to be undertaken for at least five minutes, or ten minutes if possible. Concentrate on the center of the navel. Hold the image of light. Let light be held and conceived as streaming out and filling that particular area. Picture, image, a fiery *sun* at that spot. Feel the *heat* of that sun.

Then, raise your area of concentration to the region of the Heart. Here again we picture *light,* a golden light at that area. But white light is sufficient; put all your attention into the middle of the chest, to the region of the Heart, and hold the image of light in this area. Don't pay any attention to your breathing or anything else while you are doing this. Just forget about everything and hold your whole attention to the area of this center.

In the Heart, you will find a greater consciousness developing; in fact, the Heart center seems to have a consciousness all of its own, and in time you will come to learn that this consciousness and the intelligence that it gives to the person can truly be depended upon. The ideas and intelligence of the brain are quite often erroneous, but the consciousness and knowledge that the Heart will give you is always to be depended upon. It has a world of its own so to speak. Through the Heart we find a bridge to the eternal. Once there was a man who emerged from the Himalayas. He walked the length and breadth of India and to each person he said: "Thou hast a Heart." Many said: "Why don't you teach us, and tell us of other things, and expound the Scriptures?" The man said, "Just seek the Heart, all else will come." Just as Jesus said, "Seek ye first the kingdom of Heaven, and all these things shall be added unto you." So we concentrate on the Heart and image light there.

Then we raise our attention to the throat area. Again concentrate all your attention at this region. If in the beginning it will help to concentrate your attention, you can touch these regions with one or two fingers and hold your fingers there so that it gives you a feeling in these areas. Again image *light* at the throat region.

Now raise your attention to the third eye center—between and behind the root of the nose—and here again you hold your attention without deviating and again picture *light.* After this, then, you go to the top of the head, to the soft-spot area, and concentrate; picture light at the top of the head, holding the image of a great white light there, as though there were a great Sun shining at this area, at the very top of the head.

Through doing these exercises and practices, you will gradually awaken and develop these particular centers of consciousness and in time you will find that you have made additions to your person: capacities, abilities and powers not now dreamed of as being at all possible. You can become a *Superman*. These abilities will grow and appear like the blade of grass or the leaves on trees. As you practice, the powers just grow.

MANTRAS

Mantra is an Asian word relating to sound. Throughout the world, with every people, in every land, down through the history of man, the use of sound (i.e. seed words, seed sounds) has been used in the processes of inner, or psychic, development. Sound is used in this way in India, China, Egypt, Africa and among the American Indians. Certain definite sounds are utilized for the sensitizing and developing of our psychic centers. Therefore we will employ the science of mantras in our effort toward psychic development.

In India, they make use of a group of sounds in chants. Likewise they do this in Africa, the Indies, and elsewhere. Each one of these sounds has a developing vibratory action on the particular psychic center to which that particular sound is related. Our words, our language, are actually based upon the meanings of sounds of the letters in the alphabet in the original development of language. So in the use of sounds, we make use of the vowel and other sounds which have an effect upon the respective psychic center in our body.

In India, we find the following group of sounds or sound-words used daily. They should be used night and morning, every day. I will give here, now, the first sound that you use, and each one of the following as it is given. The first is "A" as in AHM or AUM, as it is written; it is pronounced as in the words "father," "what," and "water." You chant this as "AAAAAAAAA-UU-mmm." Draw out the "A" sound long and then closing with the "m" sound. Do this "A" sound, the AUM, for the twenty-one times, then follow with "OM," again drawing out the "O" and repeat for twenty-one times. This "O" sound is pronounced as in the words "home," "roam," "comb," "oh," etc. The next sound that is intoned is "U" as pronounced in the words "who," "room," "whom," "boom." Repeat it twenty-one times. Draw it out the same way as mentioned above, saying "HUUUUUUUUU-mm." Take a deep breath and hold for only a few seconds before intoning each of these sounds. This is a very spiritual sound and a sound that develops and awakens the Heart center.

Then follows the sound "E," pronounced as in the word, "nay," "may," "say," "made," "raid." Repeat twenty-one times. Draw out the "E," like "EEEEEEEEE-mmm." Then chant the sound "I," pronounced as in the words "weed," "seen," "keen," "peace" the same number of times. Draw out as "IIIIIIII-mmm." After doing all these particular sounds, one may then follow with the Buddhist mantra OM MANI PADME HUM. Give the Latin sounding of these words at all times, as for the above mantra, OHM, "OOOOOOOOO-mmm" (*O* sounded as above), "MAAAAAAAAA, NIIIIIIII, PAAAAAAAAAd, MEEEEEEEEE, HUUUUUUUUU-mmm." Remember the sounds are pronounced as explained above, the *Latin* soundings. The Buddhist mantra OM MANI PADME HUM should be repeated forty-nine times. This is a very harmonious chant. It is quite uplifting and affects your psychic and spiritual nature and psychic centers quite extraordinarily.

Disregard any other way you have heard this mantra said. It is vastly and grossly mispronounced by the uninformed.

After these two sets of mantras have been used, follow with the Egyptian sound. The Egyptian sound as given here was used by the Egyptians to "open the door," so to speak. In other words, it has an action on a particular center known as the *door,* the psychic door. They described the word in the Egyptian language as symbolic of opening the gate of the Temple. The sound is embodied as if it were the letter "F," immediately followed by the sound of "TH," as in the word "through" or "with," then followed with the sound of "A," the "A" sound having the pronunciation of A as in "father" as explained above. This is followed by the sound of "F," with "A" again sounded after the "F." Next you intone the sound of "R," follow with "A," then follow with the sound of "D" and after this, then, with the final sound "A." It is said in this way: "F T H - t h - th-th-th-th A A A A A A A A A F F A A A A A A, RRRRRRRRRAAAAAAAAADAAAAAA," this sound to be repeated twenty-one times. You should definitely feel certain centers of your body responding to this sound. It will in time open the gateway to the inflow of energy and the opening of the door of your temple. These mantras are to be chanted and used twice a day, morning and night. The "F" sound is given a very short duration so that you glide right from the "F" sound into the "TH" sound, and then into the "A;" after drawing out the "TH" sound some, draw out the "A," then say the "F" and draw out the "A" again, but not so much as the first "A." Then with the "R": draw it out some, the "A" again to be drawn out about as long as the first "A" in the first word, then the "D" and the second "A" drawn out but not so long, just a short drawing-out.

You will find that in doing these particular sounds you will enhance psychic development to a great extent. Some schools specialize in and make use of these sounds for their entire system of development. Do these particular sounds and they will actually make you ready for the practice of Astral projection, which will come later. They will make it easier, and in fact the "opening of the door" is the means and the *modus operandi* of your acquiring the ability to project.

BREATHING EXERCISES

The first requirement is to choose a posture bestowing a stern, erect seat, one that is comfortable and will not become tiring or painful. This can be done either on a proper cushion or chair of satisfactory height or, if you are able, by assuming the yoga posture.

We should understand that the term "breathing practices" does not mean the various ridiculous ways of breathing often associated with body movements, nor has it to do with deep breathing or what some may speak of as "life breaths," "vital breaths," "health breaths," "solar breaths," "vitalic breaths," or any other kind of foolish procedures or inventions as found in many books and writings by Westerners.

The breathings we are dealing with have to do with *prana.* Because of the fact that there is no English equivalent for the satisfactory translation of the word, we will keep the use of the word *prana.* This practice is called *pranayama,* therefore is not something about breathing as such. Breathing, indeed, has very little to do with it, if anything. Breathing is only one of the many exercises through which we get to the real *pranayama,* which means the "control of prana."

According to the philosophy of India, the whole universe is composed of two materials, one of which they call *akasha.* It is the omnipresent, the all-penetrating substance. Everything that has form, everything that is the result of combination is evolved out of this *akasha*. It is the akasha that becomes the air, that becomes the liquids, that becomes solids. It is the akasha that becomes the sun, the earth, the moon, the stars and the comets, and it is the akasha that becomes the human body and plants and all things that exist. It cannot be perceived; it is so subtle that it is beyond ordinary perception. It can only be seen when it has become gross—when it has taken form.

At the beginning of creation, there was only this akasha. At the end of a cosmic cycle, the solids, liquids, and gases all "melt" again into akasha. The next creation similarly proceeds out of this akasha.

By what power is this akasha manufactured into this universe? By the power of *prana*; just as akasha is the infinite, omnipresent material of this universe, so is this *prana* the infinite, omnipresent, manifesting power of this universe. At the beginning and end of a cycle everything is just akasha. All the forces that are in the universe are then resolved back into *prana*. In the next cycle, out of this prana is evolved everything that we call energy, everything that we call force. It is the prana that is manifesting as motion. It is the prana that is manifesting as gravitation, as magnetism, as nerve currents, as thought force. From thought down to the lowest force, everything is a manifestation of prana. The sum total of all the forces in the universe, mental and physical, when resolved back to their original state, is called prana. When there is neither aught nor naught, when darkness covers darkness, what exists then? That akasha existed without motion. The physical motion of the prana is stopped but it existed all the same. At the end of the cycle the energy is now displayed in the universe, where it is quieted down and becomes merely potential. At the beginning of the next cycle, it starts up, strikes upon the akasha and out of the akasha evolve these various forms. As the knowledge and control of this prana is really what is meant by pranayama, this opens to us the door to almost unlimited power.

Suppose, for instance, a man understood the prana perfectly and could control it. What power on earth would not be his? He would be able to move the sun and stars out of their places, to control everything in the universe, from the atoms to the biggest sun, because he controlled the prana. This is the end and aim of pranayama.

When a yogi becomes perfect, there will be nothing in nature not under his control. If he orders the gods, or the souls of the departed, they will come at his bidding. All the forces of nature will obey him as slaves. When the ignorant see the powers of the yogi, they call them miracles.

One peculiarity of the Hindu mind is that it always inquires for the last possible generalization, leaving the details to be worked out afterwards. The question is raised in the Vedas; "What is that, knowing which, we shall know everything?" Thus all philosophies and all books that have been written have been only to prove that, by knowing which everything is known.

If a man wants to know this universe, bit by bit, he must know every individual grain of sand, which means infinite time. He cannot know all of it. Then how can knowledge be? How can it be possible for a man to be all-knowing through particulars? The yogis say that behind this particular manifestation, there is generalization. Behind all particular ideas stands a generalized and abstract principle. Grasp it and you have grasped everything—just as this whole universe has been generalized in the Vedas into that one absolute existence, and he who has grasped that existence has grasped the whole universe. So all forces have been generalized in this prana, and he who has grasped prana has grasped all the forces of the universe, mental or physical. He who has controlled the prana has controlled his own mind and all the minds that exist. He who has controlled the prana has controlled his body and all the bodies that exist, because prana is the generalized manifestation of force.

How to control the prana is the one idea of pranayama. All the training and exercises in this regard are for that one end. Each man must begin where he stands. He must learn how to control the things that are nearest to him. This body is nearest to us, nearer than anything in the external universe. This mind is nearest of all. The prana which is working under this mind and body is the nearest to us of all the prana of the universe. This little wave of the prana which represents our own energies, mental and physical, is the nearest to us of all the waves of the infinite ocean of prana. If we can succeed in controlling this little wave, then we can hope to control the whole of prana. The yogi who has done this gains perfection. No longer is he under any power; he becomes almost almighty, almost all-knowing.

We see sects in every country who have attempted to control prana. In America we have the mind healers, the faith healers, the spiritualists, the Christian Scientists, the hypnotists, and so forth. If we examine their different teachings, we shall find at the back of them all this control of the prana, to a degree, whether they know it or not. If you boil all their theories down, what is left will be that. It is the one and the same force they are manipulating. Unknowingly they have stumbled on the discovery and are using it unconsciously without knowing its nature—but it is the same force as the yogi uses, which comes from prana.

Now for the practice of prana breathing. The first exercise that you should take up is one of merely measured breathing. Through both nostrils, breathe in and out to the count of four or six in an equal fashion. Breathe

in through both nostrils, breathe out through both nostrils.
Do this for five minutes at a time, twice a day—morning and
night. In this practice you will find that it becomes restful
to the body and nerves. It is conducive to relaxation and
peacefulness of the mental and nervous energies.
WARNING—BEWARE! I warn you, *do not* take up the
advanced breath exercises given forthwith until you have
practiced each exercise for the indicated length of time.
You are playing with dynamite if you do. Don't be a fool;
don't think you are too good or too advanced for this
admonition. In pranayama you are dealing with the most
powerful force in the Universe, that force being more than
just Vital Energy. It is actually Power, Force, ultimate
Energy. To skip some of the earlier exercises and go to the
advanced is inviting sickness, insanity, death.

The Channel must become *opened* to increase a flow
of energy into the body. For the body to receive this
energy before it is ready is to invite disaster. *I* went
through this and know certain results that come from
following directions. I am glad I didn't think I was smart
and rush or jump ahead. What I experienced, as it was, was
stupendous. I have known people who reaped disaster.

After doing this practice for a week, we then take up
the more advanced type of the practice. At the beginning
of the second week, we sit down and take our posture,
having the belt or clothing loose about the abdomen. Close
the *right* nostril, breathe *in* through the *left* nostril to the
count of four. Breathe *out,* right away, through the *right*
nostril, keeping the left nostril closed, to the count of
four. Breathe *out,* right away, through the *left* nostril,
keeping your right nostril closed, to the count of eight.
Then the new cycle—*in* through the *left, out* through the
right, in through the *right, out* through the *left, in* through
the *left,* and so on continuing this cycle, counting *four* for
each *inhalation,* counting *eight* for each *exhalation.* Do

this practice for five minutes at a time. After two weeks, this practice is to be changed—*not before.*

It doesn't matter which finger closes the nostril. Some over-fastidious "Teachers" will say hold the hand thus and so. All one has to do is close the nostril with SOME finger, even his fist if he wishes. It's like some elements of society or authorities saying one should drink tea with the little finger of the cup hand held with a slight bend, thusly!

Now you continue the breathing practice the same as before—breathing *in* through the *left* nostril, keeping the right nostril closed, to the count of four, only now, *hold* the breath *in* to the count of sixteen. Then breathe *out* through the right, closing the left nostril, to the count of eight, still holding the left nostril closed; breath *in* through the right to the count of four, hold the breath in to the count of sixteen, then breathe *out* through the *left* to the count of eight, keeping the right nostril closed; continuing to hold the right nostril closed, breathe right away back *in* through the *left* to the count of four, *hold* in for the count of sixteen, close the left nostril and breathe *out* through the *right* to the count of eight; continuing to hold the left nostril closed, breathe *in* right away through the *right* to the count of four, and so on, continuing in this pattern for five minutes, twice a day, night and morning. This second phase of the breathing practice is also performed this way for two weeks.

Now take up the third phase of the breathing. Breathe in and out starting with the left nostril to the respective counts of four and eight for the inhalation and exhalation, but now after breathing *out* each time, *hold out* the breath for the count of sixteen, *not* holding *in* as above, but otherwise doing the breathing practice as given. Do this likewise twice a day, five minutes, morning and night, for two weeks.

The fourth phase of the breathing is done as above, always starting with the *left* nostril, but now you *hold in* for the count of sixteen, as in the foregoing instructions, and also *hold out* to the count of sixteen. You *hold in* each time after breathing *in*, and you *hold out* each time after breathing *out*, holding for the count of sixteen for each held breath. You do this breathing method this way from here on, five minutes each time, twice a day, morning and night.

After you have reached the fourth phase of the pranayama breathing exercise, follow the exercise with what is known as KHUMBAKA, or suspension of breath. Khumbaka must *not* be started until you have reached the last phase of the alternate breathing, as given above. Breathe in ordinarily through both nostrils, then suddenly expel the breath and *hold* it *out* for as long as is comfortable; breathe in through both nostrils, then continue breathing normally for one minute. Then repeat; suddenly expel the breath and hold it out for as long as you can. Perform this exercise no more than four times at a sitting, twice a day.

Continuing with these last two breathing practices will lead to amazing benefits and abilities. This is in itself a terrific means of developing psychic powers.

USING A MIRROR

We have all heard of the use of crystal balls and the development of clairvoyance by the use of crystal gazing. The crystal is not the best medium for this purpose. For one thing the crystal is quite expensive to get in the proper size needed; it also has certain disadvantages in the use for development of clairvoyance.

You can also employ what is known as the magic mirror, which is a little, concave device with a black background. These are far less expensive and can also be purchased easily. Also, one can actually get quite good results with them. However, you will find the ordinary mirror—just a simple, plain, cheap mirror that anybody can get—is far better. It is larger, it gives better results, you can see much more clearly, and your images are greater in size due to the larger instrument. The use of the mirror has been employed along with the crystal down through the ages. You hear the old story in children's storybooks; "Mirror, mirror on the wall"—and then a command to the mirror was given. Then we have the stories about Merlin and his magic mirror that he looked into. You find various people all over the world who have used the mirror in their efforts to develop clairvoyance.

The size of the mirror is not too important. One such as is found in stores, about 1½ to 2 feet high and 12 to 15 inches wide, is sufficient. A larger one will also do.

The first time your author ever used a mirror for this purpose, a letter appeared in the mirror, wherein the whole page was read. Two days later the letter was received. So, it is much more advantageous, much cheaper, and more satisfactory to employ a mirror for this purpose.

In the use of the mirror, certain preparations are necessary. You want to acquire a good grade of mirror, not necessarily expensive, but one that is of good grade. Then you want a little room—the room or place you use for your development and practice is sufficient. Put the mirror on the wall, then place a little desk or stand right under the mirror. Get a little piece of white paper, cut out a bit the size of a pea and paste it in the center of the mirror so that, when sitting down in front of the mirror, the little piece of paper will match the center of your forehead, between the eyes, at the root of the nose.

After having done this, you use a candle. All the lights in the room are to be out. Use a candle large enough so that you don't have to light it every so often, or worry about it going out. Place this candle to the left side of your stand so that just a slight reflection of it lights your face in the mirror. Then sit back in your chair, a comfortable chair, and concentrate your whole attention on this white spot in the mirror. Do not let your eyes deviate in any way. Think of nothing, just hold your whole attention on this little white spot. When you begin to see things in the mirror, keep your eyes and your attention on the white spot; don't try to see with your physical eyes. You will be doing the seeing with your inner eyes, your subtle eyes. So regardless of what appears in the mirror, do not become startled or surprised. Just continue to look at this white spot. The white spot will disappear when the development in the mirror is sufficiently clear, so that the image will be seen in the mirror instead of nothing else.

Your face will disappear; you will see only the image appearing in the mirror. You might perhaps see letters,

perhaps so clearly you will actually be able to read the
words; you might see faces, or pictures of various things;
you might see someone who has passed on; you might see
someone that you know or don't know who is at a
distance. It is possible that you may see your own face
undergo a change. There is a reason for this, and it is one
way to perceive the various metamorphoses that your face
can undergo for definite reasons. In practicing the use of
the mirror, a half-hour each time, every night or every
other night, should be sufficient. In due course you will
find that you can sit down, relax and look in your mirror,
having any wish or question in your mind, and the answer
will appear in the mirror.

If your mirror is large, your images will be
correspondingly larger than what you would see in a
crystal. They will appear more clearly, and the results that
you get will be much more satisfactory than with the use
of smaller items. A good crystal of the proper size would
cost in the area of fifty dollars or more. You can get a
mirror for a few dollars.

So here again is a great and ancient method for
psychic development. You will not only have clear seeing
and be able to see things at a given time, but you will also
develop clear hearing. You will be able to smell the vision
also, or to feel all those things seen in the mirror.

So practice this, and practice and practice. Do not be
discouraged in your endeavors, for with the use of all these
methods that are given you, you can develop into a great
psychic.

DEVELOPMENT OF WILL POWER

The exercise of a function exercises the brain or nerve center related to that function. Recognition of this relationship is the basis of techniques we can use for the development and increase of will power. For our first practice, place a candle on a desk or stand in your work or study room. Light it, and turn out the electric lights. Have a comfortable, straight-backed chair, so that you sit with your eyes about one foot to one-and-one-half feet from the candle. Look at the candle flame. See if you can see a light, an aura, around it. Keep the eyes focused on the flame and you will find that you will see a color around it. Now what are you to do? Change the color of the light, the aura of the candle flame. Concentrate, visualize a different color. With practice you will actually change the aura of the flame. You will know it to be so because others will also see the same color. So you see, you will actually be changing the vibrations of the aura. Try concentrating on *red* first. When you are once able to change the color to red, you can then easily produce any color you please.

A shoemaker friend of mine from Serbia could even change the color of a flower this way. He could also leave his body at will; I watched him levitate till his head touched the ceiling. There were other things he was able to do. His brother was able to "sleeperize" a person at a distance through mere will power. Another man I met knew what you were thinking, what you were doing and where you were, at any time he pleased. He also was able to "extract" you from your body, from a distance, whenever he pleased, if it served a constructive purpose, so that you left your physical body and were conscious in the inner body.

Next practice. You should not begin this until after you have attained some proficiency in the color-change work. Take a large bowl or vessel of water, then cut out a small square piece of paper about one fourth or one eighth inch square and float it in the center of the bowl. Place your hands on the outside of the vessel, palms toward the water. Then concentrate on the white piece of paper. After awhile you will notice it moving. The water will be moving. Do not sit close enough so that your breath will affect the water or disturb it. When you notice the paper moving, concentrate, will, command (mentally), *hold the thought* that it will move the opposite direction. Mentally think: "move to the right" or "move to the left" or "circle to the right" or "circle to the left" or "come forward" or "move backward (or away)." You will find that one day you will actually move it in the direction of your choice.

The concentration at the root of the nose likewise develops will power. So practice this concentration exercise regularly. This center is the *Energizer of Will.* The awakening of Kundalini will increase your will power.

Another exercise. Sit in the dark. Hold your hands ,or cup them, so that the fingertips are about one inch apart. Concentrate on the tips of the fingers. You will begin to see light around the fingers, then the hand. You will see sparks or a streaming of light flowing or extending out from the fingertips. In time the light will be seen to extend out and flow to the opposite fingers. This light, this aura, will increase. It will enlarge. *When* this happens, and not before, separate your fingers half an inch further apart.

Continue the practice till again the light or energy is as strong and as large as before. Then extend the distance another half inch. Repeat, increasing the distance by one inch this time. No increase in distance is to be made each time until the stream has become fully as strong and complete as in the beginning.

Then, when ready and able, you can point your finger at some object—a piece of paper for example—and command it to move or do as you will and it *shall*. The piece of paper can even be made to *leave* the water and rise up to your fingers held above it.

Practice, practice, practice.

ASTRAL PROJECTION

Astral projection is not something one should be afraid of. It is a very natural process. The astral body is merely one of the bodies every man possesses. As shown before, we have several bodies. We have ourselves (the soul) and a mind. As we come into birth, in the preparation stages, the mind and soul become clothed with a material sheath which we call the mental, or causal, body. Then when we descend to the next lower level or plane, we become clothed with another covering known as the astral body. Finally we come into the physical body, at birth, already clothed in the higher two bodies mentioned before. These various bodies are given various names amongst various people. In Egypt the astral body was known as the KA. In India, we have this body and the others involved called LINGA SHARIRA, SUKSMA SHARIRA, ANAMANI, KARANA SHARIRA, etc. But there is no point in becoming perplexed by the variety of names.

Each one of these bodies was given to us and is necessary for functioning within its respective world. Our physical body is given to us and is necessary if we are to function in this world, the physical world. The astral body is of astral matter, and is necessary for functioning in the astral world. Certainly we know we can't travel in the astral world with a fleshly body. Our causal body is required for existence and function in the mental world.

Thus, man has actually three material bodies, in each one of which he can function independently of the others.

The development of the use and function of the astral body is quite easy, and projection is really quite easy. If you carry out the practices given to you you will have no need to be frightened of leaving your physical body. Most people leave it to a small degree whenever they are asleep, or when they are given anesthesia, and so on. But the difference is that by the awakening and development of certain centers, we are able to leave and come back and retain an unbroken memory of our activity while outside our fleshly body. It has its practical uses, as you will come to learn.

The real value is primarily for spiritual or inner plane work and service, one of the necessary steps in our spiritual achievement and goal. We come to serve humanity in the inner bodies. We increase our sphere of influence, our learning, and many other things not understandable or explainable to those who have not reached this achievement.

To develop astral projection, astral travel, we lie down comfortably, relax, and quiet the breathing. After you are comfortable, put your entire attention on your feet. Try to feel the flesh, the bones, the insides of your feet. Concentrate on both feet. Try to feel all the tissues in your feet. Then concentrate on your legs and do the same there. Try to feel the warmth and the heaviness of the bones within your legs. Bring your attention up to your thighs; feel the heaviness, the bones and the flesh of your thighs. Next, put your attention on your abdomen. Relax, relax, put your whole attention on your abdomen. Try to feel all through your abdomen; then relax your chest; then go to your arms and to your hands. Feel the arms, the bones, the flesh of your arms and the weight of them on the bed. Then work on your upper arms and then your shoulders. Next put your attention on your back and feel your body lying on the bed, with all of your attention on your back. The weight of your body and your back should be felt. Then come to your neck. It is most important to relax your neck. Feel your neck, relax it, and then put your attention in your head—all through your head, all the way to your forehead, the back of your head, and up to the very top of your head.

While concentrating on each part of the body you can at the same time take a deep breath and hold it for a short period (15 seconds at a time). Mentally repeat the word "loose" while concentrating and feeling each part of your body. It would be as if you were giving your body, your parts the command: loose, loose, looser still, perfectly loose; loose, looser, looser still, perfectly loose. As you come up to each part of the body, take a deep breath, feel the part, and think these words. After doing this entire process three or four times, starting at the toes and on up to the top of the head, just relax, relax all over. Don't think; just forget about your whole body, forget about everything and put all your attention at the root of the nose or at the top of the head. Put your whole attention there— just let go. Then breathe, deeply and slowly and evenly, without paying any attention to your breathing. Breathe naturally but deeply; don't try to force yourself; never force yourself. Just keep concentrating on the root of the nose area, or at the top of the head, holding your whole attention there.

At this point one can use the Little Image or "swing" system, swinging from the root of the nose to the top of the head. Try to feel like you are on a swing, swinging back and forth, back and forth, and each time you swing up to the top of the head, try to swing higher, higher, a little more forcefully. Swing from the root of the nose in an arc to the top of the head, back and forth, harder and harder, until you fly out through the top of the head. In doing this, one day you will find you *will* fly out! You will rise above the body, and be able to look back and see your physical body, as though it were asleep, and know yourself as you are, independent of the flesh. You might even see the silver cord, the connecting cord that keeps you linked together with your physical body, but don't fear anything.

At first, when you get out of your body, try not to get too far away. Just walk around the room or within the house. As you gain in experience and strength, you can venture further out. One of the laws in astral projection is that *you are where you think,* so after awhile you will find that you merely have to think of a place or a person and you will be there. You will find yourself flying through space—or else suddenly, instantly, you are there without any sensation of having flown or "gone" through space. As you practice this, you will learn more of the laws and become more and more proficient. Above all, don't be afraid of any experience that you have while out of the body; you have the unseen protection of the Higher Self at all times. Nothing can harm you; your will is master. May you have speedy success at this endeavor.

There are some additional methods that can be added here. One method is to relax according to the technique given above, from the feet up to the head. Become thoroughly relaxed; then, with each exhalation, image an outflow of a white mist from your nose. Picture it pouring out from your nostrils, increasing and increasing with each exhalation till it forms a white cloud above your body or face. Then roll your closed eyes downward a little, as though you were looking at the point of the nose. Slow the breathing. Slower yet. Gradually make your breathing a little deeper—long, slow and deep. As you do this forget all else, keeping your thought, your consciousness, on or *in* this cloud. You will find that *you will be the cloud,* and that you are outside your body.

Never be afraid to leave, as the silver cord, your spiritual umbilical cord, keeps you attached, hooked, to your body. Therefore you must come back to it. The Bible mentions the silver cord. "Let not the silver cord be loosed, nor the Golden Bowl be broken." (Ecclesiastes 12:6).

In Ecclesiastes 7 we read: "Then shall the dust return to the earth as it was; and the spirit return unto God . . . " In this we see the Bible refers to this same silver cord, which keeps you attached to your physical body, *until the death of the Flesh body,* whereupon—when the silver cord is loosened from the body, the soul-man then leaves permanently the flesh he once wore and exists in one of the higher planes—the astral for awhile, and then the mental.

Another method is to concentrate on the solar plexus. Relax, more and more, at the solar plexus. Feel completely *loose* there; feel as though that center is opening—as though you or a cloud that is you is rising up at that area. With each deep, slow breath your weightless, cloud-like self is rising, coming out, lifting out at that area.

Or: sit in a chair, or lie down, and relax your body, from the feet upward to the top of the head. Then *picture* yourself *sinking* down through the top of your head, sinking down, down, down, into your head, into your body. Keep sinking. Feel the sensation you get when you are on an elevator and it is descending rapidly. *Feel* this sensation of sinking into your body. You will find yourself *out* of your body.

These are the various locations from which you can leave the physical body: solar plexus, back of the head, root of the nose, center of the brain and top of the head.

You can give a command yourself, when falling asleep, to awaken in your inner body. Here one can utilize that well-known law of psychology, the conditioned reflex, to enable you to leave the physical body. Another law, mentioned previously, is that where the mind is, there *you* are. A law of the higher planes is: to think is to *be*.

One thing that you may not as yet fully understand is that we merely transfer or project consciousness to the body that corresponds to the plane you want to go to. In other words, astral projection is merely a transference of consciousness to the astral body.

Now in performing this method, you will project in a rather natural way by traveling a preselected route "out" and back. Pick out a route to follow and stick to that route until you master it. So first we select our "trip" route. Look about your home. Pick out a spot to start from and a spot to go to, like from your bedroom to the kitchen or the living room. Also, map out the routy involved in getting to your destination. After selecting your route, get to know it thoroughly, physically. This means that you must walk over it many times, looking at it and getting every detail of it in your memory. Notice every little thing. Memorize the whole route area. Do everything possible to fix the route in your mind. In addition, select four to six points along the route that have some special characteristic about them—picture, a spot, a crack, a chair, anything characteristic. You can also use symbols placed at selected areas, or colors, or things with different ssmells, like peppermint, camphor, vanilla, violet, rose, etc.

After you have prepared the route in this way, and have become well acquainted with it by traversing it physically (take plenty of time to do the preliminary work) and smelling the various scents at their respective places, then lie down, relax, and recall each spot in memory. Mentally go through your route to each spot and return. Then *image* yourself rising out of your body, that is *see* your image doing this. Get your image to the first spot, then make the attempt to transfer your consciousness over into the image at that spot. Try to see, feel, smell, or hear through the image. Hold your consciousness in this image, and go through to your other selected spots and then back. One day you will find yourself *in* the image, there, at the spot. Do not become startled! Always stay calm and poised in your astral work.

IDA & PINGALA CURRENTS

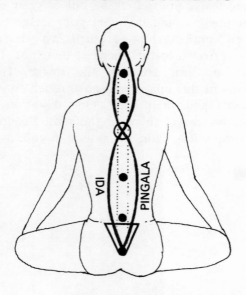

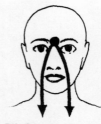

PINGALA IDA

*NOTE:—IN ANATOMY BOOKS IT IS MENTIONED THAT A FIBRE IS FOUND TO EXTEND FROM THE AREA BEHIND & BETWEEN THE EYES (BEHIND THE ROOT OF THE NOSE), IN THE HYPOPHESES STRUCTURE, DOWN TO THE TIP OF THE SPINE. ALSO, A BRANCH IS FOUND COMING FROM THE EAR AREA, CONJOINING WITH THE FIBRES AT THE HYPOPHESES AREA.

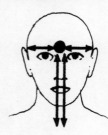

LEFT NOSTRIL CONNECTED TO IDA: RIGHT NOSTRIL CONNECTED TO PINGALA

THE AWAKENING OF KUNDALINI

According to the yogis, there are two nerve currents in the spinal column called IDA and PINGALA, and a hollow canal, which they name "Susumma;" the Greeks called it SPIEREMA, "running through the spinal cord." At the lower end of the hollow canal is what the yogis call the "Lotus of the Kundalini." They describe it as triangular in form; in it, in the symbolic language of the yogi, there is the coiled-up power of the Kundalini. When that Kundalini awakens, it tries to force a passage through this hollow canal. As it rises step by step, layer after layer, as it were, the mind becomes open and all the different visions and wonderful powers come to the yogi. When it reaches the brain, the yogi becomes perfectly detached from the body and the mind. The soul finds itself free.

We know that the spinal cord is composed in a peculiar manner. If we take the figure eight horizontally, there are two parts which are connected in the middle. Suppose you add eight after eight after eight piling one on top of the other; that will represent the spinal cord. The left is IDA and the right is PINGALA, and the hollow canal that runs through the center of the spinal cord is the SUSUMMA. All three meet and unite at the very bottom.

Where the spinal cord ends in some of the lumbar vertebrae, a fine fiber issues downward and the canal continues to run on even into that fiber, only much finer. The canal is closed at the lowest end, which is situated in what is called the sacral plexus—which, according to modern physiology, is triangular in form. The different plexuses that have their centers in the spinal canal correspond to the different lotuses or chakras of the yogi.

The yogi conceives of several subtle centers (the chakras) beginning with the *muladhara*, or the basic triangular center, and ending with the *sahasrara*, the thousand-petaled lotus in the brain. Note here that it is said to be *in* the brain. Most if not all Western writers and "authorities" take this to mean *the* brain. But this is not so. It says *in* the brain, therefore it is not meant that the housand-petalled lotus *is* the brain. Logically this could not be either, inasmuch as the brain is an organ of material sensory function and the thousand-petalled Lotus is of psychic and spiritual function. (Recent researches have found an area at the top of the brain that is *different* from the "grey matter." When you do the prescribed exercises, or other Hindu, Buddhist, Taoist, Suti, etc. practices, you will open a center at the top of the head by which new energy is contacted, confirming this fact for you.) So if we take these different plexuses as representing these lotuses, the ideas of the yogis can be understood very easily in the language of modern physiology.

We know that there are two sources of action in these nerve currents, one afferant and one efferant, one sensory and one motor; one carries a sensation to the brain and the other from the brain to the outer body. These vibrations are all connected with the brain in the long run. Several other facts will have to be remembered in order to clear the way for the explanation which is to come.

The spinal cord ends at the brain with what is called the pons, a bulb-like organ at the base of the medulla, which is said not to be attached to the brain but floating in a fluid in the brain, which amongst other reasons, serves to act as a shock protection for this organ—an important fact to remember. The pons is the container of master nerve centers that control such vital functions of the body as breathing, heartbeat, etc.

Secondly, of all the centers you should particularly remember three: the *muladhara*, which is the basic center, the *manipura*, or lotus of the navel, and the *sahasrara* in the brain. The muladhara is the repository, the generator, of Kundalini. The manipura is the "Gateway" taught of in all occult literature. All esoteric schools make use of this center in a dynamic way to increase the energies that must be manipulated. The sahasrara has been called a "door" through which another energy is contacted. It is the point of Samadhi—the source of Spiritual Illumination.

Now we take one fact from physics. We hear of electricity and various other forces connected with it. Electricity is associated with motion. Molecules composing matter are acted upon by electricity. They are usually moving in particular patterns. If all the molecules in a room, or an object, are made to move in one direction it will make a gigantic battery. Another point of physiology to remember is that the center that regulates the respiratory system, the breathing system, has a sort of controlling action over the system of nerve currents. Now we shall see why breathing is practiced.

In the first place, from rhythmical breathing comes a tendency for all the molecules in the body to move in one direction. When mind changes into will, the nerve currents are changed into a motion similar to electricity. The nerves show polarity under the action of electric currents, showing in turn that when the will is transformed the nerve currents are changed into something like electricity. Therefore when all the molecules of a body have become perfectly rhythmic, the body has become a gigantic battery of will. This gigantic, this tremendous will is exactly what the yogi wants. There is therefore a physiological explanation of the breathing exercises. They tend to bring a rhythmic action into the body and help the respiratory center to control the other centers.

At the base of the spine, in the Sacral area, there is a small canal-like anular area, a section of bone actually having three and one half coils. Then in the sixth venticle is the hollow space running through the center of the spinal cord. Since all else in the yogic teachings has been confirmed now in Western science, we must presume that likewise it may be demonstrated that this channel is closed at the lower end where it joins the anular canal. It is for this reason that the energy accumulated, or generated there, cannot rise upward until the closure is opened. But, even after this is opened, one must *increase* the *inflow*, and this is where the Solar Plexus area (actually the navel area) comes in. That's why it is called the "Gateway."

It is interesting to note that peoples throughout the world have drawn the Serpent as standing up, as illustrated here, and that the spine looks just like the serpent rising up.

It is also interesting that the base of the spine is the *only* place in the entire body where all nerve systems unite in a common meeting place. The sympathetic, the vagus, and the cerebro-spinal nerves, all anastomose at the base of the spine. The closure of the channel in the base of the spine explains why students who perform certain practices without the proper preparation can suffer injury or even death! If the energy is increased, where is it to go? It must go somewhere! If "downward" it makes a sexual excess; if through the vagus or sympathetic nerves it produces disease; if up the spine into the brain, insanity.

The aim of pranayama here is to rouse the coiled-up power in the muladhara called the Kundalini. Everything we see or dream or imagine we have to perceive in space, which is called *mahakasha*. Whenever a yogi reads the

THE SERPENT AND THE SPINAL CORD

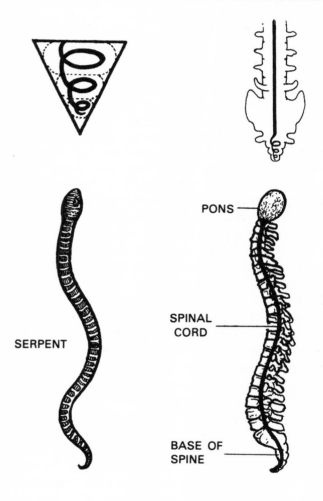

SERPENT

PONS

SPINAL
CORD

BASE OF
SPINE

thoughts of other men or perceives supersensuous objects he sees them in another sort of space called the chittakasha, the mental space. When Kundalini is aroused and enters the spinal canal, the *sushumna*, all the perceptions are in the mental space. When it has reached the end of the canal which opens out into the brain, the objectless perception is in the knowledge space. Think of "space" as relating to the word "Akasha," and you will better understand these concepts.

The Ida and Pingala are the main channels through which these currents pass. If you can make the current pass through the sushumna in the middle of the spinal cord, you have solved the problem. The sushumna in ordinary people is closed up at the lower extremity; no action passes through it. The yogi proposes a practice by which it can be opened and the nerve currents made to travel through it. When a sensation is carried to a center, the center reacts. Now the center where all the residual sensations are stored up is the muladhara, the root recepticle, and the coiled-up energy is the Kundalini, as mentioned above. It is very probable that the residual motor energy is also stored up in the same center, after deep study or meditation on external objects the part of the body where the muladhara center is situated and gets heated up. If this coiled-up energy is aroused and made active and consciously made to travel up the sushumna, it acts upon center after center and a tremendous reaction will set in. When a minute portion of energy travels along a nerve fiber, it causes a reaction from the center of perception and you have either dream or imagination. The power of long, internal meditation acts upon the vast mass of energy that is stored up, and if some of it travels along the sushumna and strikes the centers, the reaction is tremendous and immensely superior to the reaction of dream or imagination. A supersensuous perception occurs.

When it reaches the metropolis of all, in the brain, the whole area reacts, and causes a full blaze of illumination, the perception of Self. As the Kundalini force travels from center to center, the mind as it were opens up and the universe is perceived by the yogi in the fine causal form.

Now for the practice for the awakening of the Kundalini and the opening up of the closure at the base of the spine. It is because of this closure of the spine that this energy cannot rise up the spine. Occasionally, under various circumstances, a little gets through and then a person has a superconscious experience, or a slight amount of illumination, or even genius.

Now to awaken the Kundalini, we utilize the pranayama practice that you have already been given, the fourth phase of the pranayama practice—only with each breathing *in* through the left nostril, you send a mental current down through the IDA, down the left side of the spine to the sacral basic center of the Kundalini, the muladhara, striking it violently in your imagination. Then when you exhale the breath through the other nostril you picture or imagine the bringing of that current *up* through the center of the spine, through the sushumna, up into the head. When you breathe through the right nostril, you send the current down through the *right* side of the spine, through the Pingala, striking again the muladhara violently; hold the concentration there as you were taught in doing this fourth phase of the pranayama, and again bring the current up the sushumna, the center of the spine. The mental effort of sending a strong, electricity-like power-current down your spine with each of the breaths—Ida, down the left side, and Pingala down the right—and the holding of the thought down on the muladhara and then bringing it up the center of the spine, along with the breathing, is conducive to the awakening of the Kundalini energy.

When doing the khumbaka (after doing the breathing in and out regularly and normally through both nostrils and suddenly holding the breath out), hold the breath out and put all your attention on the muladhara. Concentrate all of your mind, your thinking, your thoughts, your feelings on the muladhara.

Another exercise that helps to awaken the Kundalini is to sit and contract the rectal region as strongly as you can and hold that contraction tension in the rectal region. While holding the concentration and the contraction on the muladhara in the rectum area, attempt to lift yourself off the floor. This should be done while sitting on the floor with your legs crossed. Put your hands on the floor, and as you concentrate with the contraction of your muscles and nerves in the rectal region, try to lift yourself off the floor and hold yourself up for the count of ten, then let yourself down. Relax a minute and then repeat. Do this lifting exercise with the contraction ten times, twice a day. Thus you will find that the Kundalini will one day awaken. These two practices—of sending the current down the spine and up, and then the Khumbaka with the tension and contraction and the lifting exercise—all together go to open this channel and awaken the Kundalini. It is the awakening of the Kundalini that makes further achievements become possible.

CONCLUSION

Many books have been written; many people have hungered and sought, but only a rare few have found. In this book I have endeavored to present methods whereby one can practice and achieve certain results. If you practice diligently and intelligently, you will draw the attention of a Higher One who will come to instruct you further, be he in the flesh or on the mental plane. The instructions given herein are age-old, proven, and effective. There is no experiment, nothing fancy. The experiences to be gained have been achieved by others before you. It matters not that one may disbelieve any of it. Buddha has said that one doesn't have to believe, may even disbelieve, but only *do* what he taught and the results will be achieved anyway. A Truth doesn't depend on acceptance by anyone, by so-called authorities, or taught by any "ism" or organized body of belief. Neither is a fact made non-existent by one's disbelief. None of the results will come with a will-o-the-wisp effort. It takes years.

First practice concentration by anapana sati and/or the Hang So technique. Then, *after* you have acquired this ability, take up meditation. In procedure one should start with the breathing practice, then the Mantras, the Center development, and conclude with Meditation. The isometric exercises should be performed prior to the breath practices. Astral projection is something which you will not be ready for until you have practiced for some long while. It, like other results, is an acquirement from the practices. There must be an orderly sequence. Now you have the Keys to Spiritual Illumination. You have only to actually *do* what is prescribed!

APPENDICES

The following material has been included to help many students with alternate and additional practices leading to psychic self-development.

THE MASTER CHAKRAS
*Throb thine with Nature's throbbing heart
and all is clear from East to West.*

Emerson

The following instructions are actually a course of concentration covering, even for the most positive or steadfast of readers, a period of three or four years. With some, the results may be almost "instantaneous."

First a bit of philosophy. Our first duty in life is to be true to ourselves. If we are true to ourselves, we shall be false to no one. One must do as one's higher nature craves. We should never follow our lower nature. Freedom is doing the right thing, thinking or acting according to the highest motivations. This aids in leading you upward. However, do not fight the lower nature, or negative thoughts. If you do, the law of Reversed Effort then is set into motion. The more you deny a thing, the worse it becomes. Gain control. First you have Natural control, secondly Conscious control; finally you achieve Divine control.

Do you really want true joy, true happiness, true freedom? You can have these things. You can have the joy of the Self. You can discover this joy when you become stabilized in your own Self. What must we do to come up to this level? Upraise the Self by the Self! Upraise the lower by the Higher. Raise your consciouness up, and all the centers will open themselves. It's up to you entirely.

THE SPINAL CENTERS AND THE VENTRAL PLEXI

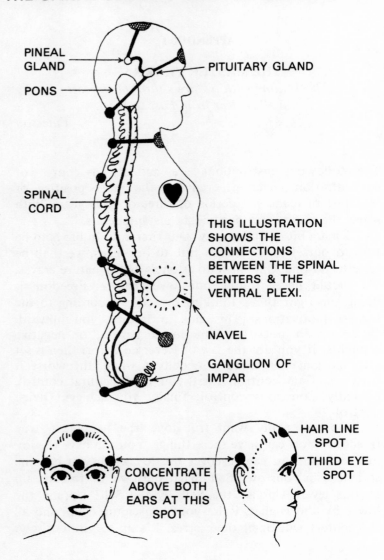

PINEAL GLAND

PITUITARY GLAND

PONS

SPINAL CORD

THIS ILLUSTRATION SHOWS THE CONNECTIONS BETWEEN THE SPINAL CENTERS & THE VENTRAL PLEXI.

NAVEL

GANGLION OF IMPAR

HAIR LINE SPOT

THIRD EYE SPOT

CONCENTRATE ABOVE BOTH EARS AT THIS SPOT

The power and the force are within you. We must make ourselves spiritual, and then we will radiate this spirituality from within. That which is within will lift us upward.

The first thing to do is concentration. Practice and develop this ability by *watching the breath*. Watch your inhalation and exhalation, not breathing unnaturally but just assuming the role of a witness of life's function inside you. Put your attention at the "nose-door" and just watch it as it comes in and out. This will cause you to notice that you have a consciousness, that you are something above life itself. Later you shall feel and hear that inner throb within you of which Emerson spoke. You become a mere observer. With the watching of the breath, you at the same time, with the incoming of the breath, *mentally* repeat *"So"* ("O" like in "boat") and as the breath comes out of it's own accord, mentally repeat *"Hang"* ("A" as in father, water, far). This concentration period is to last fifteen minutes.

Here we have the Yoga of Intelligent Will. This is the "God Yoga." It brings you to live in GOD consciously. If you change your consciousness, if you establish divine consciousness in the highest stratum of your brain, you will find the lower strata of your spine opening themselves. This sets up it's own motor effects and opens up, in due course, the lower centers. So establish consciousness at the highest level.

Continue the concentration practice for six months or so. Or, if you have arrived at this stage mentioned—that of being a witness—then sit with spine straight, eyes closed, body relaxed; put your attention, to begin with, on the area *right above the ears,* both ears. If you see things, have "visions," don't accept them. Continue on as a witness, with mind, attention, and consciousness held to the area indicated *right* above both ears. The more you concentrate here, the more relaxed you feel, the more calm. *Keep awake.* You will begin to feel the ebb and flow of life, the Universal throb. It will bring peace. Eventually you will want to sit in this posture and practice for hours and hours. This will open up some of the higher brain centers. Practice for fifteen to thirty minutes, even an hour.

When (but not before) this happens, put your attention in like manner on just the *right* ear—at the *top* of the right ear. Continue this for four or five months, your sessions occupying the same length of time. Lights will come, darkness will come, then an even greater light and a beautiful melodious hum. Listen to it silently. You can then close both ears and listen. Now you will have healing powers in you. You should allow thirty minutes to a session at least.

The next step is to concentrate between the two eyes. You may see a flood of light of various colors. Keep concentrating. Continue for one to one and a half years at this area. A huge dark spot will come. Keep concentrating on the dark spot. Then out of the dark spot will come a greater light than seen before. You are very advanced now, but there is a long way to go yet. You have only conquered the animal in you.

The next step is to put your attention to the hair line, at the forehead, above the third eye center. Continue for an indefinite time, thirty or more minutes to a session. In time you will be taught a further practice, in this wise:

SERENE I FOLD MY HANDS AND WAIT,
NOR CARE FOR WIND NOR TIDE NOR SEA;
I RAVE NO MORE 'GAINST TIME OR FATE,
FOR, LO! MY OWN SHALL COME TO ME.

APPENDIX II

SENSORY CONCENTRATION

In the system of concentration on the senses, we have a method that helps in the development of concentration as well as sensitizing and developing the astral senses.

To begin with, we take an object of any kind and fix the eyes on it for awhile. Take exact note of the shape, color and other features present. Then close the eyes and endeavor to remember or imagine the object plastically in exactly the same form, color, etc. as in reality. If it vanishes from your imagination, recall it again. In the beginning you may be successful for only a few seconds, but persevere. Repeat the exercise, and you will find that the object recalled appears more and more distinct. Do not be discouraged by initial failures. When starting this practice do not exercise longer than ten minutes, but gradually extend it up to one half hour, little by little. The purpose of the exercise is accomplished when you can hold on to an image without interruption for five minutes.

When you have arrived at this point, you may pass on to imagining objects with your eyes open. The objects ought to give the impression of being suspended in the air and be visible before the eyes, even to the point of seeming tangible.

After the visual concentration, perform the exercise of auditory concentration. Imagine the ticking of a clock, continuing with this day to day, so that you hear the clock more and more distinctly. Later you can practice hearing the noises of a running brook. Do not in either case allow any pictorial imagination.

Then go to sensory concentration. Produce the sensation of cold, warmth or some other sensation and continue this exercise day by day, till the sensation can be continued for five minutes. No visual or auditory imagination should be combined with this. When you have acquired faculty of concentration to such a degree as to produce any sensation chosen, and hold onto it for five minutes without interruption, you may continue with the next practice.

This practice involves olfactory concentration. Imagine the scent of roses, violets, lilacs or another perfume and hold on to this aroma without picturing the flower. This likewise must be continued until you can achieve five minutes of uninterrupted perception of the chosen aroma.

Next comes taste concentration. Choose some taste—sour, sweet, bitter, etc.—and practice day after day until you can continue the taste sensation continuously for five minutes.

APPENDIX III

"MAGNET" DEVELOPMENT

In the East, a frequent practice is the use of a magnet. A bar magnet is suspended above the crown of the head. A horseshoe type magnet will not work for this purpose. Experiment, and you will learn the pole to have adjacent to your crown area. Then take your position and sit right under the magnet at the given area, continuing thusly for up to one half hour. The particular polarity produces an expanding effect, a stimulating influence upon the crown center and pineal body. This leads to clairvoyance. At first one may have diverse sensations: a drawing, pulling pulsating, uplifting, or expanding feeling. One might even feel effects throughout the body; shoots or shafts of light may be seen, or tiny stars. Dizziness may be felt; colors may be seen. Let all these things come and be continued for the specified time. It will be well worth your while.

USING THE BAR MAGNET

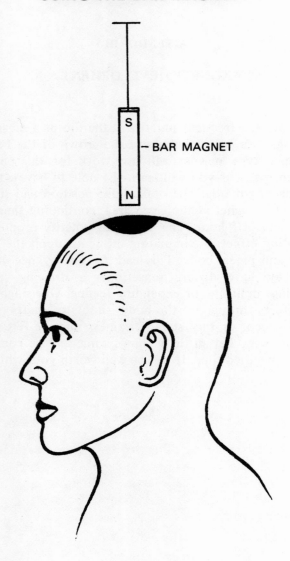

BAR MAGNET

APPENDIX IV

SOLAR PLEXUS DEVELOPMENT

Archimedes said: "Show me one point in the Universe and I shall lift the globe off its hinges."

It is not generally realized that in saying this he revealed and concealed a great occult mystery, namely the secret of the Fourth dimension. Here is the Secret of Space Magic!

Transferring consciousness to the center of anything, one can achieve mastery of the thing. Through this, also, the mental balance can be established at any time. This mental balance is the specific fundamental property of the mind, or causal principle. Consciousness knows no bounds. One can, consequently, learn to transfer consciousness to the farthest distance. Consciousness must become *free* of material limitations, bondage and identification. We must become identified with our inner nature instead.

Thus we will start transferring consciousness into the Fourth Dimension of the body. We will practice this as follows:

Sit in position. Transfer your consciousness into the very middle of your body, into the pit of the stomach area, the solar plexus. You must feel like a mere dot, as an atom in the center, between the spine and the frontal pit of the stomach. Try to stay there at least five minutes. Regard your body from this point. The more diminutive you image or feel yourself, the bigger you will perceive the body around you, even till you seem as big as the universe.

The easiest way to do this is to associate the shrinking process with breathing. Start by feeling yourself as a ball of consciousness, in, through, and around your body. Then, with each inhalation, feel smaller, shrink in diameter. Keep shrinking with each breath, until you feel yourself as a tiny point of consciousness, BEING, at the pit, at the very center point or in the solar plexus. While experiencing yourself existing there as a globe or ball of consciousness—Light—keep the attention centered at the navel. Feel a current entering at the navel with each breath, and feel yourself shrink. Keep shrinking till *you* are at that ONE-POINT. Hold, keep that concentration; feel yourself at the center point for five minutes. Then while continuing the breathing, but reversing the procedure, with each exhalation *enlarge* yourself—*you* as a Ball-globe of consciousness. Become larger and larger, till you are again the globe surrounding and permeating the Body. But don't stop there! Keep on, expanding, enlarging, growing greater and greater, to twice your normal circumference and eventually even more, to the capacity of your room. One can in time expand ever more and more. Buddha had a consciousness expansion of three miles. His was the greatest even among Buddhas. One should be steadfast in this practice. Continue, keep it up so that you will be feeling, actually, what is said here, not merely imagining.

APPENDIX V

PSYCHIC HEALING

The acquirement of Psychic Healing can provide us with the means of being helpful to others and increase our usefulness to man. Those who have healing abilities may have been "born" with it, but only because the particular energy was operative in their bodies. The same "born with" ability can be increased. It also can be produced and developed. It certainly isn't some "gift from God," nor is any other psychic ability.

Let's begin, then, to produce and develop psychic healing. Your first practice should be as follows: Take a large glass filled with water. Sit down holding the glass of water in front of you on a stand or table, resting your arms on same with your hands around the glass of water, but not so the fingers touch, and put your attention in the water, particularly that area between the hands. Take deep breaths, holding for a short period for about fifteen to twenty breaths only. Continue the exercise nightly for about fifteen minutes.

After performing this practice for two weeks, one can add another, that of holding the hands together with fingertips touching. Do this for ten minutes nightly in addition to the glass-holding practice. There are nerve centers in the fingertips that have to do with healing abilities; this practice develops those nerve centers.

After about a month at those two practices, one can add still another: breathing. Breathe in as in the normal manner, but with a full breath, and as you do, think "SHI" (she) and image the indrawing of Universal Healing Energy into your lungs. Exhaling, think "FI" (fee—like in *flea*, that bites) and image this energy flowing down the arms from the shoulders to the fingertips, and even outward from the fingertips as currents of Healing Energy. You will eventually be able to *see* this energy. One must *think* this activity and actually feel the Energy flowing down your arms and fingers. In time you won't have to "feel" it; you will actually feel it to the same degree as you can feel a pencil between your fingers or any other touch sensation. There are vibratory reasons for thinking *Shi* and *Fi*. (Don't think *Shi* and *Fi* as "shie" or "fye," as in "pie" or "eye" or "high." Think *ee* as in "feet.") This practice should be performed for five minutes.

The next practice is similar, but on the exhalation you concentrate on the eyes, with the eyes open, sending the Fi into and filling the eyeballs. After a week or two of this, select a spot at a distance of three to five feet, focusing the eyes on this spot while performing this aspect of the practice. In time one will be able to send a Healing Ray through the eye to a sick person. Allow five minutes for the eye aspect of a session.

APPENDIX VI

PSYCHIC PHOTOGRAPHY

In times past, there was great controversy as to the veracity and possibilities of photographing what may be called the supra mundane. But it is now proven that such can be done, has been done and is done.

It was in Boston, Massachusetts, that Mumler produced a spirit photograph in 1862. In the years following there have been thousands of similar productions, some frauds, others genuine pictures of "spirit forms."

It is known that photographic film is sensitive to rays that the human eye cannot see, as many cases have shown. There have been many photographs of the supra mundane examined and proven to be unretouched after exposure, even under exacting tests wherein there was no chance of preparing the film or faking in any way. Many tests were made in complete optical visibility, yet the film showed forms and images not visible to witnesses. Film has been used with ordinary cameras, on ordinary film, and even without use of a camera.

Closely allied to "spirit" photography is that known as thought photography. The latter is a method of capturing on film images of the thoughts of one or more people present, and even images which were scenes from far distant areas.

During the 1940's and onward, one of the most prominent spirit photographers was J. Edwards. Mr. Edwards was always willing to work before large audiences, in moderately lighted conditions and under stringent test conditions.

One may, however, not necessarily "believe in" the concepts of spiritualism in order to photograph discarnate entities. A family was visiting an old church in England and took photographs of it. One was of a choir stall. After development, the film showed all the seats filled with distinguishable forms, clothed in the dress of another time gone by. There have been many, many such photos taken, even by people who strongly disbelieved in any kind of psychic phenomena, spirits or similar realities.

Many tests include conditions whereby the film, paper and camera are never within reach of the medium or confederates, prior to the actual testing. The supplies usually are held by a member of the testing committee from the moment of purchase until the film is developed and prints made. One need not be a medium to produce supra mundane photography, contrary to what spiritualists claim and believe.

Some psychic-photography experimenters insist that good results can only be obtained by the use of infrared film. This cannot be true, since many unanticipated photos have been achieved with far less sensitive film. It appears that ordinary high-speed film used by most photographers is sensitive enough. However, for thought-form photography and where no camera is used, one may use highly sensitive contrast paper.

Those of spiritualistic temperament may sit quietly at a table, in subdued light. When communication begins, the presence should be asked if he will assist with the experiment, and certain signals should be given and adopted.

PSYCHIC PHOTOGRAPHY

FILM IS ENCLOSED IN A
SUITABLE MATERIAL & IT
CAN BE TAPED OR HELD
BY HAND TO THE
FOREHEAD. TAPING IT
WOULD BE BETTER.

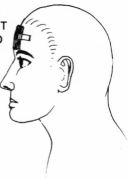

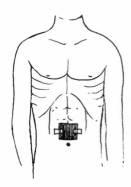

FILM OVER
SOLAR PLEXUS

When the signal is given, one of the sitters takes his place against a dark background and the "spirit" is asked to appear on the film. A signal may then be given as to when the shutter should be clicked.

Success will be achieved if this is continued patiently until the results desired are obtained. Other researchers in psychic photography claim positive results may be achieved by proceding as follows: Obtain the most sensitive film, paper and camera available. It is suggested that the most sensitive film is Eastman Kodak Company's H9R 402. This is very highly sensitive infrared film; any heating element, such as a toaster, electric heater, etc., will suffice as a light source. An electric iron is best. The camera should have a quartz crystal lens. Also, one should use a camera designed to make double exposure impossible.

One ought to acquire Major Tom Patterson's book, *Spirit Photography,* which is very helpful.

In obtaining thought pictures, one can use such a simple method as having the experimenter hold sensitive paper or film (with careful observation regarding the light conditions) against his forehead, solar plexus, or even between the palms of his hands. Have the paper or film wrapped to protect it from direct contact with the skin. The media should be held in the area selected for at least fifteen minutes. Concentration during this time must be on the object entirely, as completely as possible. In the beginning, one should use as simple an image as possible: stars, a ring of light, or any other simple, uncomplicated form. In time, one can concentrate on faces or scenes.

This is a field which can provide very interesting work, produce surprising results and even lead to unsuspected, at present, accomplishments. This method could well surpass and be even easier than the old slate writing. Begin; do persist, and may success be yours.

APPENDIX VII

THE MASS OF LIGHT METHOD

The drawing, collecting and concentration of energy from the space around you provides another very effective method of attaining psychic development. It is, like all valuable methods, not a quick way, but takes time and effort.

With this method you must first gain the ability to form a Ball of Energy. To do this, cup your hands together in front of you, arms extended one to two feet away, with your hands forming a hollow. Your wrists should be separated so that you can see into the "cup" formed by your hands. Now take a deep breath, hold for a few seconds, then pronounce *Brahma,* intoned in this manner: Brraaahmmmaaa. Draw out the "r" sound like "Brr" (it's cold!), then draw out the "Ah" like *a* in father, then the "m" sound, drawing it out like "mmm" (it's good!); then intone the "ah" sound again, drawing it out.

Repeat this over and over with each exhalation, for ten to fifteen minutes, all the while focusing your eyes and concentration into the cupped area of your hands. This practice is to be done with lights out, in the dark. You must continue this practice for as many weeks or months as it takes for the needed effect to take place, which is the condensation and formation of a Ball of Light, or light-like substance, which will form and be *seen* in the cup of your hands—a sphere or Mass of Energy seen as light, to a greater or lesser degree. *After* you have succeeded thus far,

THE "MASS OF LIGHT" METHOD

DRAWING ENERGY INTO AREA OF CUPPED HANDS

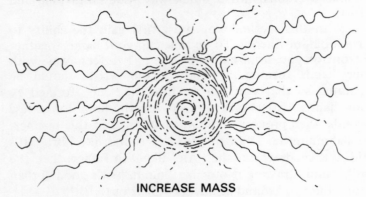

INCREASE MASS

BEFORE DRAWING ITS ENERGY
TO A PSYCHIC CENTER

you begin to augment this Mass of Energy by the use of
your eyes, the Mantra and the Will. Now, first form the
Mass in your hollow hand area; then, after it is perceived,
raise your eyes upward, say the Mantric Word and bring
your eyes downward, mentally *pulling* Energy from above
down to your hand area. Then do the same from the left
of the room, then from the right, from above, from left,
from right, over and over, pulling Energy from all parts of
the room and conjoining it to that in your cup area. The
object is to increase the Ball of Energy to twice the size,
three or even four times the size, till you have a Ball of
Energy six inches to one foot in diameter. When you
finally are able to actually accomplish this goal, put your
attention on the Ball of Light-energy and, using mental
pulling or drawing, *draw* the Energy from the Mass into
your Solar Plexus. As you draw it or invoke it to you and
into your Solar Plexus, you intone AAAHMMM, "Ah" as
in father, and drawing out the "Ah"and the "M" sounds.
(No *oo* sound is interposed between the A and M.) Keep
repeating this aspect, the chanting of the AHM and the
pulling of energy mentally to you, into your Solar Plexus,
from the Ball of Energy you have formed. You, of course,
have to form the Ball of Energy and enlarge it each time
before this drawing aspect is done. This is continued each
night for fifteen to thirty minutes. *Feel* the Energy enter
the solar plexus. (In fact, if you have performed each step
and succeeded, you *will* feel it.) Continue to pull the
energy into the solar plexus for one month, then perform
the same procedure at the Heart Center area, then the
Throat Center, the Eye Center and finally the Top of the
Head. For the Eye and Top of the Head Center, one
should of course form the Ball at the head level or just
above it. By this time, you won't need to use your hands
as a focalizing area. This is a very effective and powerful

practice. Doing it is the only way that you will discover its truth and the value and results it brings.